Mahanirvana , antra

Tantra of the Great Liberation

(Sir John Woodroffe)

[1913]

This book has been published by:

Contact: sales@nuvisionpublications.com

URL: http://www.nuvisionpublications.com

Publishing Date: 2007

ISBN# 1-59547-911-2

Please see my website for several books created for education, research and entertainment.

Specializing in rare, out-of-print books still in demand.

Table of Contents

Introduction and Preface

The Tantra has been assigned to the group of sixty-four known as those of the Rathakranta. It was first published by the Adi-Brahma-Samaja in 1798 Shakabda (A.D. 1876), and was printed in Bengali characters, with the notes of the Kulavadhuta Shrimad Hariharananda Bharati under the editorship of Anandachandra Vidyavagisha. The preface to this edition stated that three MSS. were consulted; one belonging to the library of the Samaja; the second supplied by Durgadasa Chandhuri, and the third taken from the library of Raja Ram Mohun Roy. This text appears to be the basis of subsequent publications. It was again printed in 1888 by Shri Krishna Gopala Bhakta, since when there have been several editions with Bengali translations, including that of Shri Prasanna Kumara Shastri. The late Pandit Jivananda Vidyasagara published an edition in Devanagari character, with the notes of Hariharananda; and the Venkateshvara Press at Bombay have issued another in similar character with a Hindi translation.

The second portion of the manuscript in his possession contained over double the number of Shlokas to be found in the first part here published.

The edition which has been used for the translation is that (now out of print) edited and published at Calcutta by Shri Krishna Gopala Bhakta in Chaitra 1295 Bengali era (April, 1888), with Commentary of Shrimad Hariharananda Bharati, and with additional notes by the learned and lately deceased Pandit Jaganmohana Tarkalangkara, called Vriddha in order to distinguish him from another celebrated Pandit of the same name. A new edition of the same work is now, in course of publication, with further notes by the latter's son, Pandit Jnanendranatha Tantraratna.

In conclusion, I wish to thank my Indian friends for the aid they have given me in the preparation of this and other kindred works, and to whom I am indebted for much information gathered during many pleasant hours which we have spent together in the study of a subject of common interest to them and myself. The Tantras generally are written in comparatively simple Sanskrit. For their rendering, however, a

7

working knowledge of their terminology and ritual is required, which can be only fully found in those to whom it is familiar through race, upbringing, and environment, and in whom there is still some regard for their ancient inheritance. As for others, they must learn to see through the Indian eye of knowledge until their own have been trained to its lines of vision. In this way we shall be in the future spared some of the ridiculous presentments of Indian beliefs common in the past and even now too current.

ARTHUR AVALON.

Mount Kailasa

And in the regions beyond rises Mount Meru, centre of the world-lotus. Its heights, peopled with spirits, are hung with clusters of stars as with wreaths of Malati flowers. In short, it is written: "He who thinks of Himachala, though he should not behold him, is greater than he who performs all worship in Kashi (Benares). In a hundred ages of the Devas I could not tell thee of the glories of Himachala. As the dew is dried up by the morning sun, so are the sins of mankind by the sight of Himachala."

After a description of the mountain, the Dialogue opens with a question from Parvvati in answer to which and those which succeed it, Shiva unfolds His doctrine on the subjects with which this particular Tantra deals.

Shiva and Shakti

Guna

The Worlds (Loka)

Inhabitants of the Worlds

Varna

Ashrama

Correspondence Between Macrocosm and Microcosm

The Ages

The Scriptures of the Ages

The Human Body

The Five Sheaths

Anna-Maya Kosha

Prana-Maya Kosha

Mano-maya, Vijñana Kosha, and Ananda-maya Kosha

Nadi

Chakra

There are six chakra, or dynamic Tattvik centres, in the body – viz., the muladhara, svadhishthana, mani-pura, anahata, vishuddha, and ajna – which are described in the following notes. Over all there is the thousand-petalled lotus (sahasrara-padma).

Muladhara

Svadhisthana

Mani-pura

Anahata

Vishuddha

Ajna

Sahasrara Padma

The Three Temperaments

It is to be noted, however, that the Prana-toshini cites a passage purporting to come from the Mahanirvana Tantra, which is apparently in direct opposition to the foregoing:

Divya-vira-mayo bhavah kalau nasti kada-chana

Guru and Shishya

Initiation

Diksha

Abhisheka

Sadhana

Worship Generally

Forms of Achara

9

Mantra

The Gayatri Mantra

Yantra

Mudra

Sandhya

Puja

Yajna

Vrata

Tapas

Japa

Sangskara

Purashcharana

Bhuta-shuddhi

Nyasa

These actions on the body, fingers, and palms also stimulate the nerve centres and nerves therein.

Panchatattva

Chakrapuja

Yoga

Shodhana: Shatkarmma

Dridhata: Asana

Sthirata: Mudra

Dhairya: Pratyahara

Laghava: Pranayama

Pratyaksha: Dhyana

Nirliptatva: Samadhi

Forms Of Samadhi Yoga

Shatchakra-bheda

Sin and Virtue

Karmma

Four Aims Of Being

Dharmma

Kama

Artha

Moksha

Siddhi

A. A.

Chapter 1

Questions relating to the Liberation of Beings

THE enchanting summit of the Lord of Mountains, resplendent with all its various jewels, clad with many a tree and many a creeper, melodious with the song of many a bird, scented with the fragrance of all the season's flowers, most beautiful, fanned by soft, cool, and perfumed breezes, shadowed by the still shade of stately trees; where cool groves resound with the sweet-voiced songs of troops of Apsara, and in the forest depths flocks of kokila maddened with passion sing; where (Spring) Lord of the Seasons with his followers ever abide (the Lord of Mountains, Kailasa); peopled by (troops of) Siddha, Charana, Gandharva, and Ganapatya. It was there that Parvati, finding Shiva, Her gracious Lord, in mood serene, with obeisance bent low and for the benefit of all the worlds questioned Him, the Silent Deva, Lord of all things movable and immovable, the ever Beneficent and ever Blissful One, the nectar of Whose mercy abounds as a great ocean, Whose very essence is the Pure Sattva Guna, He Who is white as camphor and the Jasmine flower, the Omnipresent One, Whose raiment is space itself, Lord of the poor and the beloved Master of all yogi, Whose coiled and matted hair is wet with the spray of Ganga and (of Whose naked body) ashes are the adornment only; the passionless One, Whose neck is garlanded with snakes and skulls of men, the three-eyed One, Lord of the three worlds, with one hand wielding the trident and with the other bestowing blessings; easily appeased, Whose very substance is unconditioned Knowledge; the Bestower of eternal emancipation, the Ever-existent, Fearless, Changeless, Stainless, One without defect, the Benefactor of all, and the Deva of all Devas.

Shri Parvati said:

O Deva of the Devas, Lord of the world, Jewel of Mercy, my Husband, Thou art my Lord, on Whom I am ever dependent and to Whom I am ever obedient. Nor can I say ought without Thy word. If Thou hast affection for me, I crave to lay before Thee that which passeth in my mind. Who else but Thee, O Great Lord, in the three worlds is able to solve these doubts of mine, Thou Who knowest all and all the Scriptures.

Shri Sadashiva said:

What is that Thou sayest, O Thou Great Wise One and Beloved of My heart, I will tell Thee anything, be it ever so bound in mystery, even that which should not be spoken of before Ganesha and Skanda Commander of the Hosts of Heaven. What is there in all the three worlds which should be concealed from Thee? For Thou, O Devi, art My very Self. There is no difference between Me and Thee. Thou too art omnipresent. What is it then that Thou knowest not that Thou questionest like unto one who knoweth nothing.

The pure Parvati, gladdened at hearing the words of the Deva, bending low made obeisance and thus questioned Shangkara.

Shri Adya said:

O Bhagavan! Lord of all, Greatest among those who are versed in Dharmma, Thou in former ages in Thy mercy didst through Brahma reveal the four Vedas which are the propagators of all dharmma and which ordain the rules of life for all the varying castes of men and for the different stages of their lives. In the First Age, men by the practice of yaga and yajna prescribed by Thee were virtuous and pleasing to Devas and Pitris. By the study of the Vedas, dhyana and tapas, and the conquest of the senses, by acts of mercy and charity men were of exceeding power and courage, strength and vigour, adherents of the true Dharmma, wise and truthful and of firm resolve, and, mortals though they were, they were yet like Devas and went to the abode of the Devas. Kings then were faithful to their engagements and were ever concerned with the protection of their people, upon whose wives they were wont to look as if upon their mothers, and whose children they regarded as their very own. The people, too, did then look upon a neighbour's property as if it were mere lumps of clay, and, with devotion to their Dharmma, kept to the path of righteousness. There were then no liars, none who were selfish, thievish, malicious, foolish, none who were evil-minded, envious, wrathful, gluttonous, or lustful, but all were good of heart and of ever blissful mind. Land then yielded in plenty all kinds of grain, clouds showered seasonable rains, cows gave abundant milk, and trees were weighted with fruits. No untimely death there was, nor famine nor sickness. Men were ever cheerful, prosperous, and healthy, and endowed with all qualities of beauty and brilliance. Women were chaste and devoted to their husbands. Brahmanas, Kshatriyas, Vaishyas, and Shudras kept to and followed the customs, Dharmma, yajna, of their respective castes, and attained the final liberation.

After the Krita Age had passed away Thou didst in the Treta Age perceive Dharmma to be in disorder, and that men were no longer able by Vedic rites to accomplish their desires. For men, through their anxiety and perplexity, were unable to perform these rites in which much trouble had to be overcome, and for which much preparation had to be made. In constant distress of mind they were neither able to perform nor yet were willing to abandon the rites.

Having observed this, Thou didst make known on earth the Scripture in the form of Smriti, which explains the meaning of the Vedas, and thus delivered from sin, which is cause of all pain, sorrow, and sickness, men too feeble for the practice of tapas and the study of the Vedas. For men in this terrible ocean of the world, who is there but Thee to be their Cherisher, Protector, Saviour, their fatherly Benefactor, and Lord?

Then, in the Dvapara Age when men abandoned the good works prescribed in the Smritis, and were deprived of one half of Dharmma and were afflicted by ills of mind and body, they were yet again saved by Thee, through the instructions of the Sanghita and other religious lore.

End of the First Joyful Message, entitled "Questions relating to the Liberation of Beings."

Chapter 2

Introduction to the Worship of Brahman

HAVING heard the words of the Devi, Shangkara, Bestower of happiness on the world, great Ocean of mercy, thus of the truth of things spoke.

Sadashiva said:

O Exalted and Holy One! Benefactress of the universe, well has it been asked by Thee. By none has such an auspicious question been asked aforetime. Worthy of all thanks art Thou, Who knoweth all good, Benefactress of all born in this age, O Gentle One! Thou art Omniscient. Thou knowest the past, present, and future, and Dharmma. What Thou hast said about the past, present, and future, and, indeed, all things, is in accordance with Dharmma, and is the truth, and is without a doubt accepted by Me. O Sureshvari! I say unto you most truly and without all doubt that men, whether they be of the twice born or other castes, afflicted as they are by this sinful Age, and unable to distinguish the pure from the impure, will not obtain purity or the success of their desired ends by the Vedic ritual, or that prescribed by the Sanghitas and Smritis. Verily, verily, and yet again verily, I say unto you that in this Age there is no way to liberation but that proclaimed by the Agama. I, O Blissful One, have already foretold in the Vedas, Smritis, and Puranas,' that in this Age the wise shall worship after the doctrine of the Agama. Verily, verily, and beyond all doubt, I say to you that there is no liberation for him who in this Age, heedless of such doctrine, follows another. There is no Lord but I in this world, and I alone am He Who is spoken of in the Vedas, Puranas, and Smritis and Sanghitas. The Vedas and the Puranas proclaim Me to be the cause of the purity of the three worlds, and they who are averse to My doctrine are unbelievers and sinners, as great as those who slay a Brahmana. Therefore, O Devi! the worship of him who heeds not My precepts is fruitless, and, moreover, such an one goes to hell. The fool who would follow other doctrine heedless of Mine is as great a sinner as the slayer of a Brahmana or of a woman, or a parricide; have no doubt of that.

In this Age the Mantras of the Tantras are efficacious, yield immediate fruit, and are auspicious for Japa, Yajna, and all such practices and ceremonies. The Vedic rites and Mantras which were efficacious in the First Age have ceased to be so in this. They are now as powerless as snakes, the poison-fangs of which are drawn and are like to that which is dead. The whole heap of other Mantras have no more power than the organs of sense of some pictured image on a wall. To worship with the aid of other Mantras is as fruitless as it is to cohabit with a barren woman. The labour is lost. He who in this Age seeks salvation by ways prescribed by others is like a thirsty fool who digs a well on the bank of the Jahnavi, and he who, knowing My Dharmma, craves for any other is as one who with nectar in his house yet longs for the poisonous juice of the akanda plant. No other path is there to salvation and happiness in this life or in that to come like unto that shown by the Tantras. From my mouth have issued the several Tantras with their sacred legends and practices both for Siddhas and Sadhakas. At times, O My Beloved! by reason of the great number of men of the pashu disposition, as also of the diversity of the qualifications of men, it has been said that the Dharmma spoken of in the Kulachara Scriptures should be kept secret. But some portions of this Dharmma, O Beloved! have been revealed by Me with the object of inclining the minds of men thereto. Various kinds of Devata and worshippers are mentioned therein, such as Bhairava, Vetala, Vatuka, Nayika, Shaktas, Shaivas, Vaishnavas, Sauras, Ganapatyas, and others. In them, too, are described various Mantra and Yantra which aid men in the attainment of siddhi, and which, though they demand great and constant effort, yet yield the desired fruit. Hitherto My answer has been given according to the nature of the case and the questioner, and for his individual benefit only.

None before has ever questioned Me as Thou hast done for the advantage of all mankind – nay, for the benefit of all that breathes, and that, too, in such detail and with reference to the Dharmma of each of the different Ages. Therefore, out of My affection for Thee, O Parvati! I will speak to Thee of the essence of essences and of the Supreme. O Deveshi! I will state before Thee the very essence distilled from the Vedas and Agamas, and in particular from the Tantras. As men versed in the Tantras are to other men, as the Jahnavi is to other rivers, as I am to all other Devas, so is the Mahanirvana Tantra to all other Agamas.

O Auspicious One! of what avail are the Vedas, the Puranas, or the Shastras, since he who has the knowledge of this great Tantra is Lord of all Siddhi?. Since Thou hast questioned Me for the good of the world, I will speak to Thee of that which will lead to the benefit of the universe.

O Parameshvari! should good be done to the universe, the Lord of it is pleased, since He is its soul, and it depends on Him. He is One. He is the Ever-existent. He is the Truth. He is the Supreme Unity without a second. He is Ever-full and Self-manifest. He is Eternal Intelligence and Bliss. He is without change, Self-existent, and ever the Same, Serene, above all attributes. He beholds and is the Witness of all that passes, Omni-present, the Soul of everything that is. He, the Eternal and

Omnipresent, is hidden and pervades all things. Though Himself devoid of sense, He is the Illuminator of all the senses and their powers. The Cause of all the three worlds, He is yet beyond them and the mind of men. Ineffable and Omniscient, He knows the universe, yet none know Him. He sways this incompre-hensible universe, and all that has movement and is motionless in the three worlds depends on Him; and lighted by His truth, the world shines as does Truth itself. We too have come from Him as our Cause. He, the one Supreme Lord, is the Cause of all beings, the Manifestation of Whose creative Energy in the three worlds is called Brahma. By His will Vishnu protects and I destroy, Indra and all other Guardian Devas of the world depend on Him and hold rule in their respective regions under His command. Thou His supreme Prakriti art adored in all the three worlds. Each one does his work by the power of Him who exists in his heart. None are ever independent of Him. Through fear of Him the Wind blows, the Sun gives heat, the Clouds shower seasonable rain, and the Trees in the forest flower.

There is none other but Him to meditate upon, to pray to, to worship for the attainment of liberation. Need there is none to trouble, to fast, to torture one's body, to follow rules and customs, to make large offerings; need there is none to be heedful as to time nor as to Nyasa or Mudra, wherefore, O Kuleshani! who will strive to seek shelter elsewhere than with Him?

End of the Second Joyful Message, entitled "Introduction to the Worship of Brahman."

Chapter 3

Description of the Worship of the Supreme Brahman

SHRI DEVI said:

O Deva of the Devas, great Deva, Guru of Brihaspati himself, Thou Who discourseth of all Scriptures, Mantra, Sadhana, and hast spoken of the Supreme Brahman by the adoration of Whom mortals attain happiness and liberation, do Thou, O Lord! deign to instruct us in the way of service of the Supreme Soul and of the observances, Mantra, and meditation in His worship. It is my desire, O Lord! to hear the essential substance of all these from Thee.

Shri Sadashiva said:

Listen, then, O Beloved of My life! to the most secret and supreme Truth, the mystery whereof has nowhere yet been revealed.

Because of My affection for Thee I shall speak to Thee of that Supreme Brahman, Who is ever Existent, Intelligent, and Who is dearer to Me than life itself. O Maheshvari! the eternal, intelligent, infinite Brahman may be known in Its real Self or by Its external signs. That Which is changeless, existent only, and beyond both mind and speech, Which shines as the Truth amidst the illusion of the three worlds, is the Brahman according to Its real nature. That Brahman is known in samadhi-yoga by those who look upon all things alike, who are above all contraries, devoid of doubt, free of all illusion regarding body and soul. That same Brahman is known from His external signs, from Whom the whole universe has sprung, in Whom when so sprung It exists, and into Whom all things return. That which is known by intuition may also be perceived from these external signs. For those who would know Him through these external signs, for them sadhana is enjoined.

Attend to me, Thou, O dearest One! while I speak to Thee of such sadhana. And firstly, O Adye! I tell Thee of the Mantroddhara of the Supreme Brahman. Utter first the Pranava, then the words "existence" and "intelligence," and after the word "One" say "Brahman."

18

MANTRA

This is the Mantra. These words, when combined according to the rules of Sandhi, form a Mantra of seven letters. If the Pranava be omitted, it becomes a Mantra of six letters only. This is the most excellent of all the Mantras, and the one which immediately bestows Dharmma, Artha, Kama, and Moksha. In the use of this Mantra there is no need to consider whether it be efficacious or not, or friendly or inimical, for no such considerations affect it. Nor at initiation into this Mantra is it necessary to make calculations as to the phases of the Moon, the propitious junction of the stars, or as to the Signs of the Zodiac. Nor are there any rules as to whether the Mantra is suitable or not. Nor is there need of the ten Sangskara. This Mantra is in every way efficacious in initiation. There is no necessity for considering anything else. Should one have obtained, through merit acquired in previous births, an excellent Guru, from whose lips this Mantra is received, then life indeed becomes fruitful, and the worshipper receiving in his hands Dharmma, Artha, Kama, and Moksha, rejoices both in this world and the next.

He whose ears this great jewel of Mantra reaches is indeed blest, for he has attained the desired end, being virtuous and pious, and is as one who has bathed in a the sacred places, been initiated in all Yajnas, versed in all Scriptures, and honoured in all the worlds. Happy is the father and happy the mother of such a one – yea, and yet more than this, his family is hallowed and the gladdened spirits of the Pitris rejoice with th Devas, and in the excess of their joy sing: "In our family is born the most excellent of our race, one initiate in the Brahma-mantra. What need have we now of pinda offered at Gaya, or of shraddha, tarpana, pilgrimage at holy places; of what use are alms, japa, homa, or sadhana, since now we have obtained imperishable satisfaction?"

Listen, O Devi! Adored of the world, whilst I tell You the very truth that for the worshippers of the Supreme Brahman there is no need for other religious observances. At the very moment of initiation into this Mantra the disciple is filled with Brahman, and for such an one, O Devi! what is there which is unattainable in all the three worlds?. Against him what can adverse planets or Vetala, Chetaka, Pishacha, Guhyaka, Bhuta, the Matrika, Dakini, and other spirits avail?

The very sight of him will drive them to flight with averted faces. Guarded by the Brahma-mantra, clad with the splendour of Brahman, he is as it were another Sun. What should he fear, then, from any planet? They flee, frightened like elephants at the sight of a lion, and perish like moths in a flame. No sin can touch, and none but one as wicked as a suicide can harm, him, who is purified by truth, without blemish, a benefactor of all beings, a faithful believer in Brahman. The wicked and sinful who seek to harm him who is initiate in the knowledge of the Supreme Brahman do but harm themselves, for are they not indeed in essence inseparate from the ever-existent One? For he is the holy sage and well-wisher, working for the happiness of all, and, O Devi! should it be possible to harm such an one who can go in peace? For him, however, who has no knowledge of the meaning of nor of the awakening of the Mantra, it is fruitless, even though it were inwardly uttered ten million times.

The worshipper disciple should in the like manner, with his mind well under control, perform Anga-nyasa in accordance with the rules thereof, commencing with the heart and ending with the hands.

After this, whilst reciting the Mantra Om or the Mula-mantra, Pranayama should be performed thus: He should close the left nostril with the middle of the fourth finger, and then inhale through the right nostril, meanwhile making japa of the Pranava or the Mula-mantra eight times. Then, closing the right nostril with the thumb and shutting also the mouth, make japa of the Mantra thirty-two times. After that gently exhale the breath through the right nostril, doing japa of the Mantra the while sixteen times.

In the same way perform these three acts with the left nostril, and then repeat the same process with the right nostril. O adored of the Devas! I have now told Thee of the method of Pranayama to be observed in the use of the Brahma-Mantra. The Sadhaka should then make meditation which accomplishes his desire.

DHYANA

In the lotus of my heart I contemplate the Divine Intelligence, the Brahman without distinctions and difference, Knowable by Hari, Hara, and Vidhi, whom Yogis approach in meditation, He Who destroys the fear of birth and death, Who is Existence, Intelligence, the Root of all the three worlds.

Having thus contemplated the Supreme Brahman, the worshipper should, in order to attain union with Brahman, worship with offerings of his mind. For perfume let him offer to the Supreme Soul the essence of the Earth, for flowers the ether, for incense the essence of the air, for light the Lustre of the universe, and for food the essence of the Waters of the world. After mentally repeating the great mantra and offering the fruit of it to the Supreme Brahman, the excellent disciple should commence external worship

Meditating with closed eyes on the Eternal Brahman, the worshipper should with reverence offer to the Supreme whatever be at hand, such as perfumes, flowers, clothes, jewels, food, and drink, after having purified them with the following:

MANTRA

The vessel in which these offerings are placed is Brahman, and so, too, is the gheeoffered therein. Brahman is both the sacrificial Fire and he who makes the sacrifice, and to Brahman he will attain whose mind is fixed on the Brahman by the performance of the rites which lead to Brahman. Then, opening the eyes, and inwardly and with all his power making japa with the Mula-mantra, the worshipper should offer the japa to Brahman and then recite the hymn that follows and the Kavacha-mantra. Hear, O Maheshvari! the hymn to Brahman, the Supreme Spirit, by the hearing whereof the disciple becomes one with the Brahman.

Stotra

Ong! I bow to Thee, the eternal Refuge of all:

I bow to Thee, the pure Intelligence manifested in the universe.

I bow to Thee Who in His essence is One and Who grants liberation.

I bow to Thee, the great, all-pervading attributeless One.

Thou art the only Refuge and Object of adoration.

The whole universe is the appearance of Thee Who art its Cause.

Thou alone art Creator, Preserver, Destroyer of the world.

Thou art the sole immutable Supreme, Who art neither this nor that;

Dread of the dreadful, Terror of the terrible.

Refuge of all beings, Purificator of all purificators.

Thou alone rulest the high-placed ones,

Supreme over the supreme, Protector of the Protectors.

O Supreme Lord in Whom all things are, yet Unmanifest in all,

Imperceptible by the senses, yet the very truth.

Incomprehensible, Imperishable, All-pervading hidden Essence.

Lord and Light of the Universe! save us from harm.

On that One alone we meditate, that One alone we in mind worship,

To that One alone the Witness of the Universe we bow.

21

Refuge we seek with the One Who is our sole Eternal Support,

The Self-existent Lord, the Vessel of safety in the ocean of being.

This is the five-jewelled hymn to the Supreme Soul.

He who pure in mind and body recites this hymn is united with the Brahman. It should be said daily in the evening, and particularly on the day of the Moon. The wise man should read and explain it to such of his kinsmen as believe in Brahman. I have spoken to You, O Devi! of the five-jewelled hymn, O Graceful One! listen now to the jagan-mangala Mantra of the amulet, by the wearing and reading whereof one becomes a knower of the Brahman.

MANTRA

May the Supreme Soul protect the head,

May the Supreme Lord protect the heart,

May the Protector of the world protect the throat,

May the Soul of the Universe protect my hands,

May He Who is Intelligence itself protect the feet,

May the Eternal and Supreme Brahman protect my body in all its parts always.

Salutation

Ong

I bow to the Supreme Brahman.

I bow to the Supreme Soul.

I bow to Him Who is above all qualities.

I bow to the Ever-existent again and again.

The worship of the Supreme Lord may be by body or mind or by word; but the one thing needful is purity of disposition. After worshipping in the manner of which I have spoken, the wise man should with his friends and kinsmen partake of the holy food consecrated to the Supreme Spirit. In the worship of the Supreme there is no need to invoke Him to be present or to desire Him to depart.

It may be done always and in all places. It is of no account whether the worshipper has or has not bathed, or whether he be fasting or have taken food. But the Supreme Spirit should ever be worshipped with a pure heart. After purification by the Brahma-Mantra, whatever food or drink is offered to the Supreme Lord becomes itself purifying. The touch of inferior castes may pollute the water of Ganga and the Shaligrama, but nothing which has been consecrated to the Brahman can be so polluted. If dedicated to Brahman with this Mantra, the worshipper with his people may eat of anything, whether cooked or uncooked. In the partaking of this food no rule as to caste or time need be observed. No one should hesitate to take the leavings from the plate of another, whether such another be pure or impure.

Whenever and whatsoever the place may be, howsoever it may have been attained, eat without scruple or inquiry the food dedicated to the Brahman. Such food, O Devi! even the Devas do not easily get, and it purifies even if brought by a Chamdala, or if it be taken from the mouth of a dog. As to that which the partaking of such food affects in men, what, O Adored of the Devas! shall We say of it? It is deemed excellent even by the Devas. Without a doubt the partaking of this holy food, be it but once only, frees the greatest of sinners and all sinners of their sins. The mortal who eats of it acquires such merit as can only otherwise be earned by bathing and alms at thirty-five millions of holy places. By the eating of it ten million times greater merit is gained than by the Horse-sacrifice, or indeed by any other sacrifice whatever. Its excellence cannot be described by ten million tongues and a thousand million mouths. Wherever the Sadhaka may be, and though he be a Chandala, he attains to union with the Brahman the very moment he partakes of the nectar dedicated to Him. Even Brahmans versed in the Vedanta should take food prepared by low-caste men if it be dedicated to the Brahman. No distinction of caste should be observed in eating food dedicated to the Supreme Spirit. He who thinks it impure becomes a great sinner. It would be better, O Beloved! to commit a hundred sins or to kill a Brahmana than to despise food dedicated to the Supreme Brahman. Those fools who reject food and drink made holy by the great Mantra. cause the fall of their ancestors into the lower regions, and they themselves go headlong into the Hell of blind darkness, where they remain until the Dissolution of things. No liberation is there for such as despise food dedicated to Brahman. In the sadhana of this great Mantra, even acts without merit become meritorious; in slumber merit is acquired; and acts are accepted as rightful which are done according to the worshipper's desires. For such what need is there of Vedic practices, or for the matter of that what need is there even of those of the Tantra? Whatever he does according to his desire, that is recognized as lawful in the case of the wise believer in the Brahman. For them there is neither merit nor demerit in the performance or non-performance of the customary rites. In the sadhana of this Mantra his faults or omissions are no obstacle. By the sadhana of this Mantra, O Great Devi! man becomes truthful, conqueror of the passions devoted to the good of his fellow-men, one to whom all things are indifferent, pure of purpose, free of envy and arrogance, merciful and pure of mind, devoted to the service and seeking the of his parents, a listener ever to things devine, a meditator ever on the Brahman. His mind is ever turned to the search for Brahman. With strength of determination holding his mind in close control, he is ever conscious of the nearness of Brahman. He who is initiated in the Brahma-Mantra will not lie or think to harm, and will shun to go with the wives of others. At the commencement of all rites, let him say, "Tat Sat"; and before eating or drinking aught let him say, "I dedicate this to Brahman". For the knower of Brahman, duty consists in action for the well-being of fellow-men. This is the eternal Dharmma.

I will now, O Shambhavi! speak to Thee of the duties relating to Sandhya in the practice of the Brahma Mantra, whereby men acquire that real wealth which comes to them in the form of Brahman. Wheresoever he may be, and in whatsoever posture, the excellent and well-intentioned sadhaka shall, at morning, noon and eventide, meditate upon the Brahman in the manner prescribed. Then, O Devi! let him make japa of th Gayatri one hundred and eight times. Offering the japa to the Devata, let him make obeisance in the way of which I have spoken. I have now told thee of the sandhya to be used by him in the sadhana of the Brahma-Mantra, and by which the worshipper shall become pure of heart. Listen to Me now, Thou Who art figured with grace, to the Gayatri, which destroys all sin.

Say "Parameshvara" in the dative singular, then "vidmahe," and, Dear One, after the word "Paratattvaya" say "dhimahi," adding, O Devi! the words, "tanno Brahma prachodayat."

MANTRA

"May we know the Supreme Lord; let us contemplate the Supreme Essence, and may that Brahman direct us."

This is the auspicious Brahma-Gayatri which confers Dharmma, Artha, Kama, and Moksha.

Let everything which is done, be it worship or sacrifice, bathing, drinking, or eating, be accompanied by the recitation of the Brahma-Mantra. When arising at the middle of the fourth quarter of the night, and after bowing to the Preceptor who gave initiation in the Brahma-Mantra, let it be recited with all recollection. Then obeisance should be made to the Brahman as aforesaid, after meditating upon Him. This is the enjoined morning rites. For Purashcharana, O Beautiful One! japa of the Mantra should be done thirty-two thousand times, for oblations three thousand two hundred times; for the presenting of or offering water to the Devata, three hundred and twenty times; for purification before worship thirty-two times; and Rrahmanas should be feasted four times. In Purashcharana no rule need be observed touching food or as regards what should be accepted or rejected. Nor need an auspicious time nor place for performance be selected. Whether he be fasting or have taken food, whether with or without bathing, let the Sadhaka, as he be so inclined, make sadhana with this supreme Mantra. Without trouble or pain, without hymn, amulet, nyasa, mudra, or setu, without the worship of Ganesha as the Thief, yet surely and shortly the most Supreme Brahman is met face to face

In the sadhana of this great Mantra no other Sangkalpa is necessary than the inclination of the mind thereto and purity of disposition. The worshipper of Brahman sees Brahman in everything. The worshipper does not sin, nor does he suffer harm should he perchance in such sadhana omit anything. On the contrary, if there be any omission, the use of this great Mantra is the remedy therefor. In this terrible and sinful Age devoid of tapas which is so difficult to traverse, the very seed of liberation is the use of the Brahma-Mantra. Various Tantras and Agamas have prescribed various modes of sadhana, but these, O Great Devi! are beyond the powers of the feeble men of this Age. For these, O Beloved! are short-lived, without enterprise, their life dependent on food, covetous, eager to gain wealth, so unsettled in their intellect that it is without rest, even in its attempts at yoga. Incapable, too, are they of suffering and impatient of the austerities of yoga. For the happiness and liberation of such have been ordained the Way of Brahman. O Devi! verily and verily I say to You that in this Age there is no other way to happiness and liberation than that by initiation in Brahma-Mantra; I again say to You there is no other way. The rule in all the Tantras is that that which is prescribed for the morning should be done in the morning, Sandhya thrice daily and worship at midday, but, O Auspicious One! in the worship of Brahman there is no other rule but the desire of the worshipper. Since in Brahma-worship rules are but servants and the prohibitions of other worships do not prevail, who will seek shelter in any other? Let the disciple obtain a Guru who is a knower of Brahman, peaceful and of placid mind, and then, clasping his lotus-like feet, let him supplicate him as follows:

Supplication to the Guru

O merciful one! Lord of the distressed! to thee I have come for protection: cast then the shadows of thy lotus-like feet over my head, oh thou whose wealth is fame.

Having thus with all his powers prayed to and worshipped his Guru, let the disciple remain before him in silence with folded hands. The Guru will the carefully examine the signs on and qualities of the disciple, kindly call the latter to him, and give to the good disciple the great Mantra. Let the wise one sitting on a seat, with his face to the East or to the North place his disciple on his left, and gaze with tenderness upon him. The Guru, after performing Rishi-nyasa, will then place his hand on his disciple's head, and for the siddhi of the latter make japa of the Mantra one hundred and eight times.

Let the excellent Guru, ocean of kindness, next whisper the Mantra seven times into the right ear of the disciple if he be a Brahmana, or into the left ear if he be of another caste. O Kalika! I have now described the manner in which instructions in Brahma-Mantra should be given. For this there is no need of puja, and his Sangkalpa should be mental only. The Guru should then raise the disciple, now become his son, who is lying prostrate at his lotus-feet, and say with affection the following.

Reply of the Guru

Rise, my son, thou art liberated: Be ever devoted to the knowledge of Brahman: Conquer thy passions: May thou be truthful, and have strength and health.

Let the excellent disciple on rising make an offering of his own self, money or a fruit, as he may afford. Remaining obedient to his preceptor's commands, he may then roam the world like a Deva. Immediately upon his initiation into this Mantra his soul is suffused with the Divine Being. What need, then, O Deveshi! for such an one to practise various kinds of sadhana? O Dearest One! I have now briefly told You of the initiation into the Brahma-Mantra. For such initiation the merciful mood of the Guru is alone necessary. The worshipper of the Divine Power, of Shiva, of the Sun, of Vishnu, Ganesha, Brahmanas versed in the Vedas and all other castes may be initiated.

In the use of this Brahma-Mantra, O Great Devi there are no restrictions. The Guru may without hesitation give his disciple his own Mantra, a father may initiate his sons, a brother his brothers, a husband his, wife, a maternal uncle his nephews, a maternal grand father his grandsons. Such fault as elsewhere there is in other worships, in the giving of one's own Mantra, in initiation by a father or other near relative does not exist in the case of this great and successfu Mantra. He who has heard it, however it may be from the lips of one initiate in the knowledge of Brahman, is purified, and attains the state of Brahman, and is affected neither by virtue nor sin. The householder of the Brahmanas and other castes who pray with the Brahma Mantra should be respected and worshipped as being the greatest of their respective classes.

Brahmanas at once become like those who have conquered their passions, and lower castes become equal to Brihmanas: therefore let all worship those initiate in the Brahma-Mantra, and thus possessed of Divine knowledge. They who slight them are as wicked as the slayers of Brahmanas, and go to a terrible Hell,where they remain as long as the Sun and Stars endure . To revile and calumniate a worshipper of the Supreme Brahman is a sin ten million times worse than that of killing a woman or bringing about an abortion. As men by initiation in the Brahma-Mantra become freed of all sins, so, O Devi! also may they be freed by the worship of Thee.

End of Third Joyful Message, entitled "Description of the Worship of the Supreme Brahman."

26

Chapter 4

Introduction of the Worship of the Supreme Prakriti

HAVING listened with attention to that which has been said concerning the worship of the Supreme Brahman, the Supreme Devi greatly pleased again thus questioned Shankara.

Shri Devi said:

O Lord of the Universe and Husband! I bathe with contentment in the nectar of Thy words concerning the excellent worship of the Supreme, which lead to the well-being of the world and to the path of Brahman, and gives light, intelligence, strength, and prosperity. Thou hast said, O Ocean of Mercy! that as union with the Brahman is attainable through worship of Him, so, it may be attained by worship of Me. I wish to know, O Lord! of this excellent worship of Myself, which as Thou sayest is the cause of union of the worshipper with the Brahman. What are its rites, and by what means may it be accomplished? What is its Mantra, and what the form of its meditation and mode of worship?. O Shambhu! who but Thee, great Physician of earthly ills, is fit to speak of it, from its beginning to its end, and in all its detail agreeable as it is to Me and beneficent to all humanity?.

Hearing the words of the Devi, the Deva of Devas, Husband of Parvati, was delighted, and spoke to Her thus:

Shri Sadashiva said:

Listen, O Thou of high fortune and destiny, to the reasons why Thou shouldst be worshipped, and how thereby the individual becomes united with the Brahman. Thou art the only Para Prakriti of the Supreme Soul Brahman, and from Thee has sprung the whole Universe – O Shiva – its Mother. O gracious One ! whatever there is in this world, of things which have and are without motion, from Mahat to an atom, owes its origin to and is dependent on Thee. Thou art the Original of all the manifestations; Thou art the birthplace of even Us; Thou knowest the whole world, yet none know Thee.

Thou art Kali, Tarini, Durga, Shodashi, Bhuvaneshvari, Dhumavati. Thou art Bagala, Bhairavi, and Chhinna-mastaka. Thou art Anna-purna, Vagdevi, Kama-lalaya. Thou art the Image or Embodiment of all the Shaktis and of all the Devas. Thou art both Subtle and Gross, Manifested and Veiled, Formless, yet with form. Who can understand Thee?. For the accomplishment of the desire of the worshipper, the good of the world, and the destruction of the Danavas, Thou dost assume various forms. Thou art four-armed, two-armed, six-armed, and eight-armed, and holdest various missiles and weapons for the protection of the Universe. In other Tantras I have spoken of the different Mantras and Yantras, with the use of which Thou shouldst be worshipped according to Thy different forms, and there, too, have I spoken of the different dispositions of men. In this Kali Age there is no Pashu-bhava: Divya-bhava is difficult of attainment, but the practices relating to Vira-sadhana yield visible fruit.

In this Kali Age, O Devi! success is achieved by Kaulika worship alone, and therefore should it be performed with every care. By it, O Devi! is acquired the knowledge of Brahman, and the mortal endowed therewith is of a surety whilst living freed from future births and exonerated from the performance of all religious rites. According to human knowledge the world appears to be both pure and impure, but when Brahma-jnana has been acquired there is no distinction between pure and impure. For to him who knows that the Brahman is in all things and eternal, what is there that can be impure?. Thou art the Image of all, and above all Thou art the Mother of all. If Thou art pleased, O Queen of the Devas! then all are pleased.

Before the Beginning of things Thou didst exist in the form of a Darkness which is beyond both speech and mind, and of Thee by the creative desire of the Supreme Brahman was the entire Universe born. This Universe, from the great principle of Mahat down to the gross elements, has been created by Thee, since Brahman Cause of all causes is but the instrumental Cause. It is the Ever-existent, Changeless, Omnipresent, Pure Intelligence unattached to, yet existing in and enveloping all things. It acts not, neither does It enjoy. It moves not, neither is It motionless. It is the Truth and Knowledge, without beginning or end, Ineffable and Incomprehensible.

Thou the Supreme Yogini dost, moved by his mere desire, create, protect, and destroy this world with all that moves and is motionless therein. Mahakala, the Destroyer of the Universe, is Thy Image. At the Dissolution of things, it is Kala Who will devour all, and by reason of this He is called Mahakala, and since Thou devourest Mahakala Himself, it is Thou who art the Supreme Primordial Kalika.

28

Because Thou devourest Kala, Thou art Kali, the original form of all things, and because Thou art the Origin of and devourest all things Thou art called the Adya Kali. Resuming after Dissolution Thine own form, dark and formless, Thou alone remainest as One ineffable and inconceivable. Though having a form, yet art Thou formless; though Thyself without beginning, multiform by the power of Maya, Thou art the Beginning of all, Creatrix, Protectress, and Destructress that Thou art. Hence it is, 0 Gentle One! that whatsoever fruit is attained by initiation in the Brahma-Mantra, the same may be had by the worship of Thee.

According to the differences in place, time, and capacity of the worshippers I have, O Devi! in some of the Tantras spoken of secret worship suited to their respective customs and dispositions. Where men perform that worship which they are privileged to perform, there they participate in the fruits of worship, and being freed from sin will with safety cross the Ocean of Being. By merit acquired in many previous births the mind inclines to Kaulika doctrine, and he whose soul is purified by such worship himself becomes Shiva. Where there is abundance of enjoyment, of what use is it to speak of Yoga, and where there is Yoga there is no enjoyment, but the Kaula enjoys both.

If one honours but one man versed in the knowledge of the essence of Kula doctrine, then all the Devas and Devis are worshipped – there is no doubt of that.

The merit gained by honouring a Kaulika is ten million times that which is acquired by giving away the world with all its gold. A Chandala versed in the knowledge of Kaulika doctrine excels a Brahmana, and a Brahmana who is wanting in such knowledge is beneath even a Chandala..

I know of no Dharmma superior to that of the Kaulas, by adherence to which man becomes possessed of Divine knowledge. I am telling Thee the truth, O Devi! Lay it to the heart and ponder over it. There is no doctrine superior to the Kaulika doctrine, the most excellent of all. This is the most excellent path kept hidden by reason of the crowd of Pashus, but when the Kali Age advances this pathway will be revealed.

Verily and verily I say unto you that when the Kali Age reaches the fullness of its strength there will be no Pashus, and all men on earth will be followers of the Kaulika doctrine. O Vararohe! know that when Vedic and Puranic initiations cease then the Kali Age has become strong. O Shive! 0 Peaceful One! when virtue and vice are no longer judged by the Vedic rules, then know that the Kali Age has become strong.

O Sovereign Mistress of Kaula doctrine! when the Heavenly Stream is at some places broken, and at others diverted from its course, then know that the Kali Age has become strong. O Wise One! when kings of the Mlechchha race become excessively covetous, then know that the Kali Age has become strong.

When women become difficult of control, heartless and quarrelsome, and calumniators of their husbands, then know that the Kali Age has become strong. When men become subject to women and slaves of lust, oppressors of their friends and Gurus, then know that the Kali Age has become strong. When the fertility of the earth has gone and yields a poor harvest, when the clouds yield scanty rain, and trees give meagre fruit, then know that the Kali Age has become strong. When brothers, kinsmen, and companions, prompted by the desire for some trifle, will strike one another, then know that the Kali Age has become strong. When the open partaking of flesh and liquor will pass without condemnation and punishment, when secret drinking will prevail, then know that the Kali Age has become strong.

As in the Satya, Treta, and Dvapara Ages wine and the like could be taken, so they may be taken in the Kali Age in accordance with the Kaulika Dharmma. The Kali Age cannot harm those who are purified by truth, who have conquered their passions and senses, who are open in their ways, without deceit, are compassionate and follow the Kaula doctrine. The Kali Age cannot harm those who are devoted to the services of their Guru, to the lotus of their mothers' feet, and to their own wives. The Kali Age cannot harm those who are vowed to and grounded in truth, adherents of the true Dharmma, and faithful to the performance of Kaulika rites and duties. The Kali Age cannot harm those who give to the truthful KaulikaYogi the elements of worship, which have been previously purified by Kaulika rites.

The Kali Age cannot harm those who are free of malice, envy, arrogance, and hatred, and who are firm in the faith of Kaulika dharmma. The Kali Age cannot harm those who keep the company of Kaulikas, or live with Kaulika Sages, or serve the Kaulikas. The Kali Age cannot harm those Kaulikas who, whatever they may appear outwardly to be, yet remain firm in their Kaulika Dharmma, worshipping Thee according to its doctrine. The Kali Age cannot harm those who perform their ablutions, charities, penances, pilgrimages, devotions, and offerings of water according to the Kaulika ritual.

The Kali Age cannot harm those who perform the ten purificatory ceremonies, such as the blessing of the womb, obsequial ceremonies of their fathers, and other rites according to Kaulika ritual. The Kali Age cannot harm those who respect the Kaula-tattva, Kaula-dravya, and Kaula-yogi.

The Kali Age is but the slave of those who are free of all crookedness and falsehood, men of candour, devoted to the good of others, who follow Kaulika ways. In spite of its many blemishes, the Kali Age possesses one great merit, that from the mere intention of a Kaulika of firm resolution desired result ensues. In the other Ages, O Devi! effort of will produced both religious merit and demerit, but in the Kali Age men by intention merely acquire merit only, and not demerit. The slaves of the Kali Age, on the other hand, are those who know not Kulachara, and who are ever untruthful and the persecutors of others. They too are the slaves of the Kali Age who have no faith in Kulacharas, who lust after others' wives, and hate them who are faithful to Kaulika doctrine.

In speaking of the customs of the different Ages, I have, O Gentle One! and out of love, O Parvati! truly recounted to Thee the signs of the dominance of the Kali Age. When the Kali Age is made manifest, piety is enfeebled and Truth alone remains; therefore should one be truthful. O Thou Virtuous One! know this for certain, that whatsoever man does with Truth that bears fruit. There is no Dharmma higher than Truth, there is no sin greater than falsehood; therefore should man seek protection under Truth with all his soul. Worship without Truth is useless, and so too without Truth is the Japa of Mantras and the performance of Tapas. It is in such cases just as if one sowed seed in salt earth.

Truth is the appearance of the Supreme Brahman; Truth is the most excellent of all Tapas; every act is rooted in Truth. Than Truth there is nothing more excellent. Therefore has it been said by Me that when the sinful Kali Age is dominant, Kaula ways should be practised truthfully and without concealment. Truth is divorced from concealment. There is no concealment without untruth. Therefore is it that the Kaulika-sadhaka, should perform his Kaulika-sadhana openly. What I have said in other Kaulika Tantras about the concealment of Kaulika-dharmma not being blameworthy is not applicable when the Kali Age becomes strong.

In the (First or) Satya. Age, O Devi! Virtue possessed the four quarters of its whole; in the Treta Age it lost one-quarter of its Virtue; in the Dvapara Age there was of Virtue but two quarters, and in the Kali Age it has but one. In spite of that Truth will remain strong, though Tapas and Charity become weakened. If Truth goes Virtue goes also, therefore of all acts Truth should be the abiding support. O Sovereign Mistress of the Kaula-Dharmma! since men can in this Age have recourse to Kaulika Dharmma only, if that doctrine be itself infected with untruth, how can there be liberation?. With his soul purified in every way by Truth, man should, according to his caste and stage of life, perform the following acts in the manner shown by Me: initiation, worship, recitation of Mantras, the worship of Fire with ghee, repetition of Mantras, private devotions, marriage, the conception ceremony, and that performed in the fourth, sixth, or eighth months of pregnancy, the natal rite, the naming and tonsure ceremonies, and obsequial rites upon cremation and after death. All such ceremonies should be performed in the manner approved by the Agamas.

The ritual which I have ordained should be followed, too, as regards Shraddha at holy places, dedication of a bull, the autumnal festival, on setting out on a journey, on the first entry into a house, the wearing of new clothes or jewels, dedication of tanks, wells, or lakes, in the ceremonies performed at the phases of the Moon, the building and consecration of houses, the installation of Devas, and in all observances to be performed during the day or at night, in each month, season, or year, and in observances both daily or occasional, and also in deciding generally what ought and what ought not to be done, and in determining what ought to be rejected and what ought to be adopted. Should one not follow the ritual ordained, whether from ignorance, wickedness, or irreverence, then one is disqualified for all observances, and becomes a worm in dung. O Maheshi! if when the Kali Age has become very powerful any act be done in violation of My precepts, then that which happens is the very contrary of that which is desired. Initiation of which I have not approved destroys the life of the disciple, and his act of worship is as fruitless as oblations poured on ashes, and the Deva whom he worships becomes angry or hostile, and at every step he encounters danger. Ambika! he who during the dominance of the Kali Age, knowing My ordinances, yet performs his religious observances in other ways, is a great sinner. The man who performs any Vrata, or marries according to other ways, will remain in a terrible Hell so long as the Sun and Moon endure. By his performance of Vrata he incurs the sin of killing a Brahmana, and similarly by being invested with the sacred thread he is degraded. He merely wears the thread, and is lower than a Chandala, and so too the woman who is married according to other ways than Mine is to be despised, and, 0 Sovereign Mistress of the Kaulas! the man who so marries is her associate in wrong, and is day after day guilty of the sin of going with a prostitute. From him the Devata will not accept food, water, and other offerings, nor will the Pitris eat his offerings, considering them to be as it were mere dung and pus. Their children are bastards, and disqualified for all religious, ancestral, and Kaulika observances and rites. To an image dedicated by rites other than those prescribed by Shambhu the Deva never comes. Benefit there is none either in this or the next world. There is but mere waste of labour and money.

A Shraddha performed according to other rites than those prescribed by the Agamas is fruitless, and he who performs it will go to Hell together with his Pitris. The water offered by him is like blood, and the funeral cake like dung. Let the mortal then follow with great care the precepts of Shankara. What is the need of saying more? Verily and verily I say to You, O Devi! that all that is done in disregard of the precepts of Shambhu is fruitless. For him who follows not His precepts there is no future merit. That which has been already acquired is destroyed, and for him there is no escape from Hell. O Great Ruler! the performance of daily and occasional duties in the manner spoken of by Me is the same as worshipping Thee. Listen, O Devi! to the particulars of the worship with its Mantras and Yantras, which is the medicine for the ills of the Kali Age.

End of the Fourth Chapter, entitled "Introduction of the Worship of the Supreme Prakriti."

Chapter 5

The Formation of the Mantras, Placing of the Jar, and Purification of the Elements of Worship

SHRI SADASHIVA said:

Thou art the Adya Parama Shakti, Thou art all Power. It is by Thy power that We (the Trinity) are powerful in the acts of creation, preservation, and destruction. Endless and of varied colour and form are Thy appearances, and various are the strenuous efforts whereby the worshippers may realize them. Who can describe them?. In the Kula Tantras and Agamas I have, by the aid of but a small part of Thy mercies and with all My powers, described the Sadhana and Archana of Thy appearances; yet nowhere else is this very secret Sadhana revealed. It is by the grace of this (Sadhana), O Blessed One! that Thy mercy in Me is so great. Questioned by Thee I am no longer able to conceal it. For Thy pleasure, O Beloved! I shall speak of that which is dearer to Me than even life itself. To all sufferings it brings relief. It wards off all dangers. It gives Thee pleasure, and is the way by which Thou art most swiftly obtained. For men rendered wretched by the taint of the Kali Age, short-lived and unfit for strenuous effort, this is the greatest wealth. In this (sadhana) there is no need for a multiplicity of Nyasa, for fasting or other practices of self-restraint. It is simple and pleasurable, yet yields great fruit to the worshipper. Then first listen, O Devi! to the Mantroddhara of the Mantra, the mere hearing of which liberates man from future births while yet living.

By placing "Pranesha" on "Taijasa," and adding to it "Bherunda" and the Vindu, the first Vija is formed. After this, proceed to the second (to). By placing "Sandhya" on "Rakta," and adding to it "Vama-netra" and Vindu, the second Mantra is formed. Now listen, O Blessed One! to the formation of the third Mantra.

Prajapati is placed on Dipa, and to them is added Govinda and Vindu. It yields happiness to the worshippers: After making these three Mantras add the word Parameshvari in the vocative, and then the word for Vahni-kanta. Thus, O Blessed One! is the Mantra of ten letters formed. This Vidya of the Supreme Devi contains in itself all Mantras.

33

The most excellent worshipper should for the attainment of wealth and all his desires make Japa of each or all of the first three Vijas. By omitting the first three Devi the Vidya of ten letters become one of seven. By prefixing the Vija of Kama, or the Vagbhava, or the Tara, three Mantras of eight letters each are formed.

At the end of the Mantra of ten letters the word Kalika in the vocative should be uttered, and then the first three Vija, followed by the name of the Wife of Vahni. This Vidya is called Shodashi, and is concealed in all the Tantras. If it be prefixed by the Vija of Vadhu or by the Pranava, two Mantras of seventeen letters each are formed.

O Beloved! there are tens of millions upon tens of millions, nay an hundred millions, nay countless Mantras for Thy worship. I have here but shortly stated twelve of them. Whatsoever Mantras are set forth in the various Tantras, they are all Thine, since Thou art the Adya Prakriti. There is but one sadhana in the case of all these Mantras, and of that I shall speak for Thy pleasure and the benefit of humanity.

Without Kulachara, O Devi! the Shakti-Mantra is powerless to give success, and therefore the worshipper should worship the Shakti with Kulachara rites

O Adya! the five essential Elements in the worship of Shakti have been prescribed to be Wine, Meat, Fish, parched Grain, and the Union of man with woman. The worship of Shakti without these five elements is but the practice of evil magic. That Siddhi which is the object of sadhana is never attained thereby, and obstacles are encountered at every step. As seed sown on barren rocks does not germinate, so worship without these five elements is fruitless.

Without the prior performance of the morning rites a man is not qualified to perform the others. And therefore, O Devi! I shall first speak of those which are to be performed in the morning. In the second half of the last quarter of the night the disciple should rise from sleep. Having seated himself and shaken off drowsiness, let him meditate upon the image of his Guru:

Dhyana

As two-eyed and two-armed, situate in the white lotus of the head; clad in white raiment, engarlanded with white flowers, smeared with sandal paste. With one hand he makes the sign which dispels fear, and with the other that which bestows blessings. He is calm, and is the image of mercy. On his left his Shakti, holding in her hand a lotus, embraces him. He is smiling and gracious, the bestower of the fulfilment of the desires of his disciples.

34

O Kuleshvari! the disciple should, after having thus meditated upon his Teacher and worshipped him with the articles of mental worship, make Japa with the excellent Mantra, the Vagbhava-Vija..

After doing Japa of the Mantra as best lies in his power, the wise disciple should, after placing the Japa in the right palm of his excellent Guru, bow before him, saying meanwhile the following:

Mantra

I bow to thee, O Sad-guru,
Thou who destroyeth the bonds which hold us to this world,
Thou who bestoweth the vision of Wisdom,
Together with worldly enjoyment and final liberation,
Dispeller of ignorance,
Revealer of the Kula-dharmma,
Image in human form of the Supreme Brahman.

The disciple, having thus made obeisance to his Guru, should meditate upon his Ishta-devata, and worship Her as aforesaid, inwardly reciting the Mula-mantra meanwhile. Having done this to the best of his powers, he should place the Japa in the left palm of the Devi, and then make obeisance to his Ishta-devata with the following:

Mantra

To thee I bow Who art one with, and the Supporter of, the Universe,
I bow to Thee again and yet again, the Adya Kalika, both Creatrix and Destructress.

Having thus made obeisance to the Devi, he should leave his house, placing his left foot first, and then make water, discharge his bowels, and cleanse his teeth. He then should go towards some water, and make his ablutions in the manner prescribed. First of all let him rinse his mouth, and then enter the water, and stand therein up to his navel. He should then cleanse his body by a single immersal only, and then, standing up and rubbing himself, rinse his mouth, saying the Mantra the while. That best of worshippers, the Kula-Sadhaka, should then sip a little water and say:

Mantra

Atma-tattvaya Svaha

After that he should again sip water twice, followed in each case by the

Mantras

Vidya-tattvaya Svaha.

35

Shiva-tattvaya Svaha,
respectively. Lastly, he should rinse the upper lip twice.

Then, O Beloved! the wise disciple should draw on the water the Kula-yantra with the Mantra in its centre, and do Japa over it with the Mula-mantra twelve times. Then meditating on the Water as the Image of Fire, let him offer it thrice to the Sun in his joined palms. Sprinkling it thrice over his head, let him close the seven openings therein. Then for the pleasure of the Devi he should immerse himself thrice, leave the water, dry his body, and put on two pieces of clean cloth.

Tying up his hair whilst reciting the Gayatri, he should mark on his forehead with pure earth or ashes the tilaka and tri-pundra, with a Vindu over it. Let the worshipper then perform both the Vaidika and Tantrika forms of Sandhya in their respective order. Listen while I now describe to you the Tantrika Sandhya.

After rinsing his mouth in the manner described, he should, O Blessed One! invoke into the water the Waters of the holy Rivers thus:

Mantra

O Ganga, Yamuna, Godavari, Sarasvati, Narmmada,
Sindhu, Kaveri, come into this water.

The intelligent worshipper having invoked the sacred Rivers with this Mantra, and made the angkusha-mudra, should do Japa with the Mula-mantra twelve times. Let him then again utter the Mula-mantra, and with the middle and nameless fingers joined together throw drops of that water thrice upon the ground.

He should then sprinkle his head seven times with the water, and taking some in the palm of his left hand cover it up with his right. Then inwardly reciting the Vija of Ishana, Vayu, Varuna, Vahni, and Indra four times, the water should be transferred to the right palm. Seeing (in his mind's eye) and meditating upon the water as Fire, the worshipper should draw it through the nose by Ida, expel it through Pingala (into his palm), and so wash away all inward impurity.

The worshipper should then three times dash the water (so expelled into his palm) against an (imaginary) adamant. Uttering the Astra-Mantra, let him then wash his hands. Then rinsing his mouth, oblation of water should be offered to the Sun with the following:

Mantra

Ong Hring Hangsa

To Thee, O Sun, full of heat, shining, effulgent, I offer this oblation; Svaha.

Then let him meditate morning, midday, and evening upon the great Devi Gayatri, the Supreme Devi, as manifested in her three different forms and according to the three qualities.

Dhyana

In the morning meditate upon Her in Her Brahmi form, as a Maiden of ruddy hue, with a pure smile, with two hands, holding a gourd full of holy water, garlanded with crystal beads, clad in the skin of a black antelope, seated on a Swan. At midday meditate upon Her in Her Vaishnavi form, of the colour of pure gold, youthful, with full and rising breasts, situated in the Solar disc, with four hands holding the conch-shell, discus, mace, and lotus, seated on Garuda, garlanded with wild-flowers. In the evening the Yati should meditate upon Her as of a white colour, clad in white raiment, old and long past her youth, with three eyes, beneficent, propitious, seated on a Bull, holding in Her lotus-like hands a noose, a trident, a lance, and a skull.

Having thus meditated on the great Devi Gayatri, and offered water three times in the hollow of his joined hands, the worshipper should make Japa with the Gayatri either ten or a hundred times. Listen now, O Devi of the Devas! while I out of my love for Thee recite the Gayatri.

After uttering the Mula-mantra, say "Sarvva-bhuta-nivasinyai," and then "Sarvva-svarupa" and "Sayudha" in the dative singular, as also "Savarana" and "Paratpara," and then "Adyayai, Kalikayai, te, idam arghyam: Svaha". (When the Mantra will be.)

Mantra

Hring, Shring, Kring, to the Supreme Devi. O Supreme Devi, Thou Who dwelleth in all things and Whose image all things are, Who art surrounded by attendant deities, and Who bearest arms, Who art above even the most high to Thee, Who art the Adya Kalika, I offer this oblation: Svaha.

Having offered this arghya to the Mahadevi, the wise one should make Japa with the Mula-mantra with all his powers, and then place the Japa in the left hand of the Devi. Then let the Sadhaka bow to the Devi, take such water as is needed for his worship, bowing to the water whence he has drawn it, and proceed to the place of worship, earnestly meditating on and reciting hymns of praise to the Devi meanwhile. On his arrival there let him wash his hands and feet, and then make in front of the door the Samanyarghya. The wise one should draw a triangle, and outside it a circle, and outside the circle a square, and after worshipping the Adhara-shakti place the vessel on the figure.

Let him wash the vessel with the Weapon-Mantra, and while filling it with water let him say the Heart-Mantra. Then, throwing flowers and perfume into the water, let him invoke the holy Rivers into it. Worshipping Fire, Sun, and Moon in the water of the vessel, let him say the Maya Vija over it. The Dhenu and Yoni Mudras should then be shown. This is known as Samanyarghya. With the water and flowers of this oblation the Devata of the entrance to the place of worship should be worshipped, such as Ganesha, Kshetrapala, Vatuka, Yogini, Ganga, Yamuna, Lakshmi, and Vani. The wise one, lightly touching that part of the door-frame which is on his left, should then enter the place of worship with his left foot forward, meditating the while on the lotus-feet of the Devi. Then, after worship of the presiding Deva of the site, and of Brahma in the south-west corner, the place of worship should be cleansed with water taken from the common offering. Let the best of worshippers then with a steady gaze remove all celestial obstacles, and by the repetition of the Weapon-Mantra remove all obstacles in the Anta-riksha.

Striking the ground three times with his heel, let him drive away all earthly obstacles, and then fill the place of worship with the incense of burning sandal, fragrant aloe, musk, and camphor. He should then mark off a rectangular space as his seat, draw a triangle within it, and therein worship Kama-rupa with the

Mantra

To Kama-rupa, Namah:

Then for his seat spreading a mat over it, let him worship the Adhara-Shakti with the

Mantra

Kling, Obeisance to the Adhara-Shakti of the lotus-seat.

The learned worshipper should then seat himself according to the "tied heroic" mode, with his face towards the East or the North, and should consecrate the Vijaya. (With the following)

Mantra

Ong Hring. Ambrosia, that springeth from ambrosia, Thou that showereth ambrosia, draw ambrosia for me again and again. Bring Kalika within my control. Give siddhi; Svaha.

This is the Mantra for the consecration of Vijaya. Then inwardly reciting the Mula-mantra seven times over the Vijaya, show the Dhenu, the Yoni, the Avahani, and other Mudras.

38

Then satisfy the Guru who resides in the Lotus of a thousand petals by thrice offering the Vijaya with the Sangketa-Mudra, and the Devi in the heart by thrice offering the Vijaya with the same Mudra, and reciting the Mula-mantra. Then offer oblations to the mouth of the Kundali, with the Vijaya reciting the following

Mantra

Aing (0 Devi Sarasvati), Thou Who art the Ruler of all the essences, do Thou inspire me, do Thou inspire me, and remain ever on the tip of my tongue; Svaha.

After drinking the Vijaya he should bow to the Guru, placing his folded palms over the left ear, then to Ganesha, placing his folded palms over his right ear, and lastly to the Eternal Adya Devi, by placing his folded palms in the middle of his forehead, and should the meanwhile meditate on the Devi.

The wise worshipper should place the articles necessary for worship on his right, and scented water and other Kula articles on his left. Saying the Mula-mantra terminated by the Weapon-Mantra, let him take water from the common offering and sprinkle the articles of worship with it, and then enclose himself and the articles in a circle of water. After that, O Devi! let him by the Vahni Vija surround them with a wall of fire. Then for the purification of the palms of his hands he should take up a flower which has been dipped in sandal paste, rub it between the palms, reciting meanwhile the Mantra Phat, and throw it away.

Then in the following manner let him fence all the quarters so that no obstructions proceed from them. Join the first and second fingers of the right hand, and tap the palm of the left hand three times, each time after the first with greater force, thus making a loud sound, and then snap the fingers while uttering the weapon-Mantra. He should then proceed to perform the purification of the elements of his body. The excellent disciple should place his hands in his lap with the palms upwards, and fixing his mind on the Muladhara Chakra let him rouse Kundalini by uttering the Vija "Hung." Having so roused Her, let him lead Her with Prithivi by means of the Hangsa Mantra to the Svadhishthana Chakra, and let him there dissolve each one of the elements of the body by means of another of such elements. Then let him dissolve Prithivi together with odour, as also the organ of smell, into water. Dissolve water and taste, as also the sense of taste itself, into Fire. Dissolve Fire and vision and form, and the sense of sight itself, into air.

Let air and touch, as also the sense of touch itself, be dissolved into ether. Dissolve ether and sound into the conscious Self and the Self into Mahat, Mahat itself into Prakriti, and Prakriti Herself into Brahman. Let the wise one, having thus dissolved (the twenty-four) tattvas, then think

39

of an angry black man in the left side of the cavity of his abdomen of the size of his thumb with red beard and eyes, holding a sword and shield, with his head ever held low, the very image of all sins.

Then the foremost of disciples should, thinking of the purple Vayu Vija as on his left nostril, inhale through that nostril sixteen times. By this let him dry the sinful body. Next, meditating on the red Vija of Agni as being situate in the navel, the body with all its sinful inclinations should be burnt up by the fire born of the Vija, as also by sixty-four Kumbhakas. Then, thinking of the white Varuna Vija in his forehead, let him bathe (the body which has been so burnt) with the nectar-like water dropping from the Varuna Vija by thirty-two exhalations.

Having thus bathed the whole body from feet to head, let him consider that a Deva body has come into being. Then, thinking of the yellow Vija of the Earth as situate in the Muladhara circle, let him strengthen his body by that Vija and by a steadfast and winkless gaze. Placing his hand on his heart and uttering the

Mantra

Ang, Hring, Krong, Hangsah, So'hang.
Let him infuse into his body the life of the Devi.

O Beauteous Face! the Mantras enjoined for Shad-ang-ga-nyasa are Ka-varga between Ang and Āng, Cha-varga between Ĭng and Īng, Ta-varga between Ŭng and Ūng, Ta-varga between Eng and Aing, and Pa-varga between Ong and Aung, and the letters from Ya to Ksha between Vindu and Visarga respectively, and having placed the letters according to the rules of Nyasa, the Sadhaka should then meditate upon Sarasvati:

Dhyana

I seek refuge in the Devi of Speech, three-eyed, encircled with a white halo, whose face, hands, feet, middle body, and breast are composed of the fifty letters of the alphabet, on whose radiant forehead is the crescent moon, whose breasts are high and rounded, and who with one of her lotus hands makes Jnana-mudra, and with the other holds the rosary of Rudraksha beads, the jar of nectar, and learning.

After this has been done, Rishi-nyasa should be performed. The Revealers of the Mantra are Brahma and the Brahmarshis, the metre is of the Gayatri and other forms, and its presiding Devata is the Adya Kali. The Vija is the Vija of the Adya, its Shakti is the Maya Vija, and that which comes at the end is the Kamala Vija. Then the Mantra should be assigned to the head, mouth, heart, anus, the two feet, and all the parts of the body. The passing of the two hands three or seven times over the whole body from the feet to the head, and from the head to the feet, making japa meanwhile of the Mula-mantra, is called Vyapaka-nyasa, which yields the declared result.

O Beloved! by adding in succession the six long vowels to the first Vija of the Mula-mantra, six Vidya are formed. The wise worshipper should in Angga-kalpana utter in succession these or the Mula-mantra alone, and then say "to the two thumbs," "to the two index fingers," "to the two middle fingers," "to the two ring fingers," "to the two little fingers," "to the front and back of the two palms," concluding with Namah, Svaha, Vashat, Hung, Vaushat, and Phat in their order respectively.

When touching the heart say "Namah," when touching the head "Svaha," and when touching the crown lock thereon "Vashat." Similarly, when touching the two upper portions of the arms, the three eyes and the two palms, utter the Mantras Hung and Vaushat and Phat respectively. In this manner nyasa of the six parts of the body should be practised, and then the Vira should proceed to Pithanyasa. Then let the Vira place in the lotus of the heart, the Adhara-shakti, the tortoise, Shesha serpent, Prithivi, the ocean of ambrosia, the Gem Island, the Parijata tree, the chamber of gems which fulfil all desires, the jewelled altar, and the lotus seat. Then he should place on the right shoulder, the left shoulder, the right hip, the left hip, respectively and in their order, Dharmma, Jnana, Aishvaryya, and Vairagya, and the excellent worshipper should place the negatives of these qualities on the mouth, the left side, the navel, and the right side respectively. Next let him place in the heart Ananda Kanda, Sun, Moon, Fire, the three qualities, adding to the first of their letters the sign Vindu, and the filaments and pericarp of the Lotus, and let him place in the petals of the lotus the eight Pitha Nayikas – Mangala, Vijaya, Bhadra, Jayanti, Aparajita, Nandini, Narasinghi, Vaishnavi, and in the tips of the petals of the lotus the eight Bhairavas – Asitanga, Chanda, Kapali, Krodha, Bhishana, Unmatta, Ruru, Sanghari.

Then the worshipper should, after forming his hands into the Kachchhapa Mudra, take two fragrant flowers, and, placing his hands on his heart, let him meditate upon the ever-existent Devi. The nature of meditation upon Thee, O Devi! is of two kinds, according as Thou art imagined formless or with a form. As formless Thou art ineffable and incomprehensible, imperceptible. Of Thee it cannot be said that Thou art either this or that, Thou art omnipresent, unobtainable, attainable only by Yogis through penances and acts of self-restraint. I will now speak of meditation upon Thee in corporeal form in order that the mind may learn concentration, that desires be speedily achieved, and that the power to meditate according to the subtle form may be aroused.

The form of the greatly lustrous Kalika, Mother of Kala Who devours all things, is imagined according to Her qualities and actions.

41

Dhyana

I adore the Adya Kalika Whose body is of the hue of the (dark) rain-cloud, upon Whose forehead the Moon gleams, the three-eyed One, clad in crimson raiment, Whose two hands are raised – the one to dispel fear, and the other to bestow blessing – Who is seated on a red lotus in full bloom, Her beautiful face radiant, watching Maha-Kala, Who, drunk with the delicious wine of the Madhuka flower, is dancing before Her.

After having meditated upon the Devi in this form, and placed a flower on his head, let the devotee with all devotion worship Her with the articles of mental worship. Let him offer the lotus of the heart for Her seat, the ambrosia trickling from the lotus of a thousand petals for the washing of Her feet, and his mind as arghya. Then let him offer the same ambrosia as water for rinsing of Her mouth and bathing of Her body, let him offer the essence of the ether to be raiment of the Devi, the essence of scent to be the perfumes, his own heart and vital air the essence of fire, and the ocean of nectar to be respectively the flowers, incense, light, and food offerings (of worship).

Let him offer the sound in the Anahata Chakra for the ringing of the bell, the essence of the air for the fan and fly-whisk, and the functions of the senses and the restlessness of the mind for the dance before the Devi. Let various kinds of flowers be offered for the attainment of the object of one's desire: amaya, anahangkara, araga, amada, amoha, adambha, advesha, akshobha, amatsaryya, alobha, and thereafter the five flowers – namely, the most excellent flowers, ahingsa, indriya-nigraha, daya, kshama, and jnana. With these fifteen flowers, fifteen qualities of disposition, he should worship the Devi.

Then let him offer (to the Devi) the ocean of ambrosia, a mountain of meat and fried fish, a heap of parched food, grain cooked in milk with sugar and ghee, the Kula nectar, the Kula flower, and the water which has been used for the washing of the Shakti. Then, having sacrificed all lust and anger, the cause of all impediments, let him do japa.

The mala (rosary) prescribed consists of the letters of the alphabet, strung on Kundalini as the thread. After reciting the letters of the alphabet from A to La, with the Vindu superposed upon each, the Mula-mantra should be recited. This is known as Anuloma. Again, beginning with La and ending with A, let the sadhaka make japa of the Mantra. This is known as Viloma and Ksha-kara is called the Meru.

The last letters of the eight groups should be added to the Mula-mantra, and having made japa of this Mantra of one hundred and eight letters the japa should be offered (to the Devi) with the following:

Mantra

O Adya Kali, Who abidest in the innermost soul of all, Who art the innermost light, O Mother! accept this japa of my heart. I bow to Thee.

Having finished the japa, he should mentally prostrate himself, touching the ground with the eight parts of his body. Having concluded the mental worship, let him commence the outer worship.

I am now speaking of the consecration of the Vishesh-arghya, by the mere placing whereof the Devata is exceedingly pleased. Do Thou listen. At the mere sight of the cup of this offering the Yoginis, Bhairavas, Brahma, and other Devatas dance for joy and grant siddhi. The disciple should on the ground in front of him and on his left draw with water taken from the Samanyarghya a triangle, with the Maya Vija in its centre, outside the triangle a circle, and outside the circle a square, and let him there worship the Shakti of the Adhara with the

Mantra

Hring!

Obeisance to the Shakti of the Adhara.

He should then wash the Adhara, and place it on the Mandala, and worship the region of Fire with the

Mantra

Mang!

Obeisance to the circle of Fire possessed of ten sections.

And having washed the arghya vessel with the Mantra Phat, the worshipper should place it on the Adhara with the Mantra Namah. He should then worship the cup with the

Mantra

Ang!

Obeisance to the circle of Sun who has twelve divisions;

and fill the vessel (in which the offering is made) whilst repeating the Mula-mantra three parts with wine and one part with water, and having placed scent and flower in it, he should there worship, O Mother! with the Mantra following:

Mantra

Ung!

Obeisance to the Moon with its sixteen digits.

He should then place in front of the special offering, on bael leaves dipped in red sandal paste, durva grass, flowers, and sun-dried rice.

Having invoked the holy waters (of the sacred Rivers into the arghya) by the Mula-mantra and Angkusha-mudra, the Sadhaka should meditate upon the Devi, and worship Her with incense and flowers, making japa of the Mula-mantra twelve times. After this let him display over the arghya the Dhenu Mudra and the Yoni Mudra, incense sticks and a light. The worshipper should then pour a little water from the arghya into the vessel kept for that purpose, and sprinkle himself and the offering therewith. The vessel containing the offering must not, however, be moved until the worship is concluded. O Thou of pure Smiles! I have now spoken of the consecration of the special offering. I will now pass to the principal Yantra which grants the aims of all human existence.

Draw a triangle with the Maya Vija within it, and around it two concentric circles (the one outside the other). In the space between the two circumferences of the circles draw in pairs the sixteen filaments, and outside these the eight petals of the lotus, and outside them the Bhu-pura, which should be made of straight lines with four entrances, and be of pleasing appearance. In order to cause pleasure to the Devata the disciple should (reciting the Mula-mantra the meanwhile) draw the Yantra either with a gold needle, or with the thorn of a bael tree on a piece of gold, silver, or copper, which has been smeared with either the Svayambhu, Kunda, or Gola flowers, or with sandal, fragrant aloe, kungkuma, or with red sandal paste. A clever carver may also carve the Yantra on crystal, coral, or lapis lazuli.

After it has been consecrated by auspicious rites, it should be kept inside the house; and on this being done all wicked ghosts, all apprehensions from (adverse) planets, and diseases are destroyed; and by the grace of this Yantra the worshipper's house becomes of pleasing aspect. With his children and grandchildren, and with happiness and dominion, he becomes a bestower of gifts and charities, a protector of his dependents, and his fame goes abroad. After having drawn the Yantra and placed it on a jewelled altar in front of the worshipper, and having worshipped the Devata of the Pitha according to the rules of Pitha-nyasa, the principal Devi should be adored in the pericarp of the Lotus.

I will now speak of the placing of the jar and the formation of the circle of worship by the mere institution of which the Devata is well pleased, the Mantra becomes fruitful, and the wishes of the worshipper are accomplished. The jar is called kalasa, because Vishva-karma made it from the different parts of each of the Devatas.

It should be thirty-six fingers breadth (in circumference) in its widest part, and sixteen in height. The neck should be four fingers breadth, the mouth six fingers, and the bottom five fingers breadth. This is the rule for the design of the kalasha. It should be made either of gold, silver, copper, bell-metal, mud, stone, or glass, and without hole or crack. In its making all miserliness should be avoided, since it is fashioned for the pleasure of the Devas. A kalasha of gold, one of silver, one of copper, and one of bell-metal give enjoyment, emancipation, pleasure of mind, and nourishment respectively to the worshipper. One of crystal is good for the attainment of Vashikarana, and one of stone for the attainment of Stambhana. A kalasha made of mud is good for all purposes. Whatever it is made of it should be clean and of pleasing design.

On his left side the worshipper should draw a hexagon with a point in its centre, around it a circle, and outside the circle a square. These figures should be drawn either with vermilion or Rajas (Kula-pushpa), or red sandal paste; the Devata of the support should then be worshipped thereon. The Mantra for the worship of the Shakti or Devi of the support is –

Mantra

Hring,

salutation to the Shakti of the support.

The support for the jar should be washed with the Mantra namah, and placed on the Mandala, and the jar itself with the Mantra Phat, and then placed on the support.

Let the disciple then fill the kalasha with wine, uttering meanwhile the Mula-mantra and the Matrika Varnas, with Vindu in Viloma order. The wise one who is then himself possessed of the disposition of the Devi should worship the region of Fire, Sun, and Moon in the support in the jar and in the wine in the manner already described. After decorating the jar with vermilion, red sandal paste, and a garland of crimson flowers, the worshipper should perform Panchikarana.

Strike the wine-jar with a wisp of kusha grass, saying Phat; then, whilst uttering the Vija Hung, veil it by the Avagunthana Mudra, next utter the Vaja Hring, and look with unwinking eye upon the jar, then sprinkle the jar with the Mantra Namah. Lastly, whilst reciting the Mula-mantra, smell the jar three times. this is the Panchikarama ceremony.

Making obeisance to the jar, purify the wine therein by throwing red flowers into it, and say the following:

Mantra

Ong, O Devi Sudhe! by the Supreme Brahman, Who is One without a second: and who is always both gross and subtle, destroy the sin of slaying a Brahmana which attached to thee (the wine) by the death of Kacha. O Thou Who hast Thy abode in the region of the Sun, and Thy origin in the dwelling-place of the Lord of Ocean (in the churning of which thou, O Nectar! wast produced), thou who art one with the Ama Vija, mayest Thou be freed from the curse of Shukra. O Devi! as the Pranava of the Vedas is one with the bliss of Brahman, may by that truth be destroyed Thy sin of slaying a Brahmana.

Mantra

Hring: the Supreme Hangsa dwells in the brilliant Heaven, as Vasu It moves throughout the space between Heaven and Earth. It dwells on earth in the form of the Vedic Fire, and in the Sacrificer, and is honoured in the Guest. It is in the household Fire and in the consciousness of man, and dwells in the honoured region. It resides in Truth and in the Ether.

It is born in water, in the rays of light in Truth and in the Eastern Hill where the Sun rises. Such is the great Aditya, the Truth, Which cannot be bound or concealed, the Great Consciousness Who dwelleth everywhere – Brahman.

Mantra

"Ha-Sa-Ksha-Ma-La-Va-Ra-Yung:

Salutation to Ananda-Bhairava: Vashat";

and in the worship of the Ananda-Bhairavi the Mantra is the same, except that its face is reversed, and in place of its Ear the left Eye should be placed, and then should be said:

Mantra

"Sa-Ha-Ksha-Ma-La-Va-Ra-Ying:

Salutation to the Wine Devi: Vaushat".

Then, meditating upon the union of the Deva and Devi in the wine, and thinking that the same is filled with the ambrosia of such union, japa should be made over it of the Mula-mantra twelve times. Then, considering the wine to be the Devata, handfuls of flowers should be offered with japa of the Mula-Mantra. Lights and incense-sticks should be waved before it to the accompaniment of the ringing of a bell. Wine should be always thus purified in all ceremonies, whether puja of the Devata, Vrata, Homa, marriage, or other festivals.

The disciple, after placing the meat on the triangular Mandala in front of him, should sprinkle it with the Mantra Phat, and then charge it thrice with the Vijas of Air and Fire. Let him then cover it up with the Gesture of the Veil, uttering the Kavacha-Mantra, and protect it with the Weapon-Mantra Phat. Then, uttering the Vija of Varuna, and displaying the Dhenu-Mudra, make the meat like unto nectar with the following:

Mantra

May that Devi whose abode is in the breast of Vishnu and in the breast of Shankara purify this my meat, and give me a resting-place at the excellent foot of Vishnu.

In a similar manner, placing the fish and sanctifying it with the Mantras already prescribed, let the wise one say the following Mantra over it:

Mantra

"We worship the Father of the Three; He Who causes nourishment, He Who is sweet-scented. As the fruit of the Urvaruka is detached of itself from the stalk on which it grows, so may He free us whilst living from the bond of Karmma, until we are finally liberated, and made one with the Supreme".

Then, O Beloved! the disciple should take and purify the parched grain with the following:

Mantras

Ong! As the Eye of Heaven is plainly visible to those of the common man, so do the Wise have constant vision of the Excellent Foot of Vishnu. The Intelligent and Prayerful, whose mind is awake and controlled, see the most excellent Foot of Vishnu.

Or all the Tattvas may be consecrated by the Mula-Mantra itself. To him who has belief in the root, of what use are the branches and leaves?.

I say that anything which is sanctified by the Mula-Mantra alone is acceptable for the pleasure of the Devata. If the time be short, or if the disciple be pressed for time, everything should be sanctified with the Mula-Mantra, and offered to the Devi. Truly, truly, and again truly, the ordinance of Shankara is that if the Tattvas be so offered, there is no sin or shortcoming.

End of Fifth Joyful Message, entitled "The Formation of the Mantras, Placing of the Jar, and Purification of the Elements of Worship."

Chapter 6

Placing of the Shri-patra, Homa, Formation of the Chakra, and other Rites

SHRI DEVI said:

As Thou hast kindness for Me, pray tell Me, O Lord! more particularly about the Pancha-tattvas and the other observances of which Thou hast spoken.

Shri Sadashiva said:

There are three kinds of wine which are excellent – namely, that which is made from molasses, rice, or the Madhuka flower. There are also various other kinds made from the juice of the palmyra and date tree, and known by various names according to their substance and place of production. They are all declared to be equally appropriate in the worship of the Devata.

. Howsoever it may have been produced, and by whomsoever it is brought, the wine, when purified, gives to the worshipper all siddhi. There are no distinctions of caste in the taking of wine so sanctified. Meat, again, is of three kinds, that of animals of the waters, of the earth, and of the sky. From wheresoever it may be brought, and by whomsoever it may have been killed, it gives, without doubt, pleasure to the Devas. Let the desire of the disciple determine what should be offered to the Devas. Whatsoever he himself likes, the offering of that conduces to his well-being. Only male animals should be decapitated in sacrifice. It is the command of Shambhu that female animals should not be slain. There are three superior kinds of Fish – namely, Shala, Pathina and Rohita. Those which are without bones are of middle quality, whilst those which are full of bones are of inferior quality. The latter may, however, if well fried, be offered to the Devi.

There are also three kinds of parched food, superior, middle, and inferior. The excellent and pleasing kind is that made from Shali rice, white as a moonbeam, or from barley or wheat, and which has been fried in clarified butter. The middling variety is made of fried paddy. Other kinds of fried grain are inferior. Meat, fish, and parched food,

49

fruits and roots, or anything else offered to the Devata along with wine, are called Shuddhi. O Devi! the offering of wine without Shuddhi, as also puja and tarpana (without Shuddhi), become fruitless, and the Devata is not propitiated. The drinking of wine without Shuddhi is like the swallowing of poison. The disciple is ever ailing, and lives for a short time and dies. O Great Devi! when the weakness of the Kali Age becomes great, one's own Shakti or wife should alone be known as the fifth Tattva. This is devoid of all defects. O Beloved of My Life! in this (the last Tattva) I have spoken of Svayambhu and other kinds of flower. As substitutes for them, however, I enjoin red sandal paste. Neither the Tattvas nor flowers, leaves, and fruits should be offered to the Mahadevi unless purified. The man who offers them without purification goes to hell.

The Shri-patra should be placed in the company of one's own virtuous Shakti; she should be sprinkled with the purified wine or water from the common offering. The Mantra for the sprinkling of the Shakti is –

Mantra

Aing, Kling, Sauh. Salutation to Tripura; purify this Shakti, make her my Shakti; Svaha.

If she who is to be Shakti is not already initiated, then the Maya Vija should be whispered into her ear, and other Shaktis who are present should be worshipped and not enjoyed.

The worshipper should then, in the space between himself and the Yantra, draw a triangle with the Maya Vija in its centre, and outside the triangle and in the order here stated a circle, a hexagon, and a square. The excellent disciple should then worship in the four corners of the square the Pithas, Purna-shaila, Uddiyana, Jalandhara, and Kama-rupa, with the Mantras formed of their respective names, preceded by Vijas formed by the first letter of their respective names, and followed by Namah.

Then the six parts of the body should be worshipped in the six corners of the hexagon. Then worship the triangle, with the Mula-Mantra, and then the Shakti of the receptacle with the Maya Vija and Namah. Wash the receptacle with the Mantra Namah, and then place it (as in the case of the jar) on the Mandala, and worship in it the ten parts of Vahni with the first letters of their respective names as Vijas. These parts, which are ten in number – viz., Dhumra, Archih, Jvalini, Sukshma, Jvalini, Vishphulingini, Sushri, Surupa, Kapila,Havya-kavya-vaha – should be uttered in the Dative singular, and followed by the Mantra Namah.

Then worship the region of Vahni (in the adhara or receptacle) with the following:

Mantra

Mang: Salutation to the region of Vahni with his ten qualities.

Then, taking the vessel of offering and purifying it with the Mantra Phat, place it on the receptacle, and, having so placed it, worship therein the twelve parts of the Sun with the Vijas, commencing with Ka-Bha to Tha-Da. These twelve parts are – Tapini, Tapini, Dhumra, Marichi, Jvalini, Ruchi, Sudhumra, Bhoga-da, Vishva, Bodhini, Dharini, Kshama. After this, worship the region of Sun in the vessel of offering with the following:

Mantra

Ang: Salutation to the circle of Sun, with His twelve parts.

Then the worshipper should fill the cup of offering three-quarters full with wine taken from the jar, uttering the Matrika Vijas in the reverse order. Filling the rest of the cup with water taken from the special offering, let him worship with a well-controlled mind the sixteen digits of the Moon, saying as Vijas each of the sixteen vowels before each of the sixteen digits spoken in the dative singular, followed by the Mantra Namah.

The sixteen desire-granting digits of Moon are – Amrita, Pranada, Pusha, Tushti, Pushti, Rati, Dhriti, Shashini, Chandrika, Kanti, Jyotsna, Skri, Priti, Angada, Purna, and Purnamrita. As in the case of the other Devas mentioned, the disciple should then worship the region of the Moon with the following:

Mantra

Ung: Salutation to the region of Moon with its sixteen digits.

Durva grass, sun-dried rice, red flowers, Varvara, leaf, and the Aparajita flower should be thrown into the vessel with the Mantra Hring, and the sacred waters should be invoked into it. Then, covering the wine and the vessel of offering with the Avagunthana Mudra, and uttering the Armour Vija, protect it with the Weapon-Vija, and converting it into ambrosia with the Dhenu-Mudra, cover it with the Matsya-Mudra. Making japa of the Mula-Mantra ten times, the Ishta-devata should be invoked and worshipped with flowers offered in the joined palms.

Then charge the wine with the following five Mantras, beginning with akhanda:

Mantras

O Kula-rupini! infuse into the essence of this excellent wine which produces full and unbroken bliss its thrill of joy.

Thou who art like the nectar which is in Ananga, and art the embodiment of Pure Knowledge, place into this liquid the ambrosia of Brahmananda.

O Thou, who art the very image of That! do Thou unite this arghya with the image or self of That, and having become the kulamrita, blossom in me.

Bring into this sacred vessel, which is full of wine, essence of ambrosia produced from the essence of all that is in this world, and containing all kinds of taste.

May this cup of self, which is filled with the nectar of self, Lord, be sacrificed in the Fire of the Supreme Self.

Having thus consecrated the wine with the Mantra, think of the union in it of Sadashiva and Bhagavati and wave lights and burning incense-sticks before it.

This is the consecration of the Shri-patra in Kaulika worship. Without such purification the disciple is guilty of sin, and the worship is fruitless. The wise one should then, according to the rules prescribed for the placing of the common offering, place between the jar and the Shri-patra the cups of the Guru, the cup of Enjoyment, the cup of the Shakti, the cups of the Yoginis of the Vira and of Sacrifice, and those for the washing of the feet and the rinsing of the mouth respectively, making nine cups in all.

Then, filling the cups three-quarters full of wine from the jar, a morsel of Shuddhi of the size of a pea should be placed in each of them. Then, holding the cup between the thumb and the fourth finger of the left hand, taking the morsel of Shuddhi in the right hand, making the Tattva-mudra, Tarpana should be done. This is the practice which has been enjoined. Taking an excellent drop of wine from the Shripatra and a piece of Shuddhi, Tarpana should be made to the Deva Ananda-Bhairava and the Devi Ananda-Bhairavi.

Then, with the wine in the cup of the Guru, offer oblations to the line of Gurus. in the first place to the worshipper's own Guru seated together with his wife on the lotus of a thousand petals, and then to the Parama Guru, the Parapara Guru, the Parameshti Guru successively. In offering oblations to the four Gurus, the Vagbhava Vija should first be pronounced, followed in each case by the names of each of the four

Gurus. Then, with wine from the cup of enjoyment, the worshipper should, in the lotus of his heart, offer oblations to the Adya-Kali. In this oblation Her own Vija should precede, and Svaha should follow Her name. This should be done thrice.

Next, with wine taken from the cup of the Shakti, oblation should be similarly offered to the Devata of the parts of Her body and their Avarana-Devatas. Then, with the wine in the cup of the Yogini, oblation should be offered to the Adya-Kalika, carrying all Her weapons and with all Her followers.

Then should follow the sacrifice to the Vatukas. The wise worshipper should draw on his left an ordinary rectangular figure, and after worshipping it, place therein food with wine, meat, and other things. With the Vijas of Vak, Maya, Kamala, and with the Mantra:

"Vang, Salutation to Vatuka," he should be worshipped in the East of the rectangle, and then sacrifice should be offered to him.

Then, with the

Mantra

"Yang to the Yogin is Svaha,"

sacrifice should be made to the Yoginis on the South, and then to Kshetra-pala on the West of the rectangle, with the

Mantra

"To Kshetra-pala namah,"

preceded by the letter Ksha, to which in succession the six long vowels are added with the Vindu. Following this, sacrifice should be made to Gana-pati on the North, adding to Ga the six long vowels in succession with the Vindu thereon, followed by the name of Ganesha in the dative singular, and ending with Svaha. Lastly, sacrifice should be made inside the rectangle to all Bhutas, according to proper form.

Uttering "Hring, Shring, Sarvva-vighna-kridbhyah," add "Sarvva-bhutebhyah," and then "Hung Phat Svaha;" this is how the Mantra is formed. Then a sacrifice to Shiva should be made with the following:

Mantra

Ong, O Dev! O Shiva, O Exalted One, Thou art the image of the final conflagration at the dissolution of things, deign to accept this sacrifice, and to reveal clearly to me the good and evil which is my destiny. To Shiva I bow.

This is the Mula-Mantra in the worship of Shiva.

Having said this, perform the sacrifice, saying, "This is Thy Vali. To Shiva, Namah. O Holy One! I have now described to Thee the mode of formation of the circle of worship (and the placing of the cup and other rites). Then, making with the two hands the Kachchhapa-Mudra, let the worshipper take up with his hands a beautiful fiower scented with sandal, fragrant aloes, and musk, and, carrying it to the lotus of his heart, let him meditate therein (in the lotus) upon the most supreme Adya.

Then let him lead the Devi along the Sushumna Nadi, which is the highway of Brahman to the great Lotus of a thousand petals, and there make Her joyful. Then, bringing Her through his nostrils, let him place Her on the flower (her presence being communicated) as it were, by one light to another, and place the flower on the Yantra and with folded hands pray with all devotion to his Ishta-devata thus:

Mantra

O Queen of the Devas! Thou who art easily attained by devotion. Remain here, I pray Thee, with all Thy following, the while I worship Thee.

Then, uttering the Vija Kring, say the following:

Mantra

O Adya Devi Kalika! come here with all Thy following, come here (and then say), stay here, stay here; (and then say) place Thyself here, (and then say) be Thou detained here. Accept my worship.

Having thus invoked (the Devi) into the Yantra, the Vital Airs of the Devi should be infused therein by the following pratishtha Mantra:

Mantra

Ang, Hring, Krong, Shring, Svaha; may the five Vital Airs of this Devata be here: Ang, Hring, Krong, Shring, Svaha. Her Jiva is here placed – Ang, Hring, Krong, Shring, Svaha – all senses – Ang, Hring, Krong, Shring, Svaha. Speech, mind, sight, smell, hearing, touch, and the Vital Airs of the Adya-Kali Devata, may they come here and stay happily here for ever. Svaha.

Having recited the above three times, and having in due form placed the Vital Airs (of the Devi) in the Yantra with the Lelihina-Mudra, with folded palms, he (the worshipper) should say:

Mantra

O Adya Kali! hast Thou had a good journey, hast Thou had a good journey? O Parameshvari! mayest Thou be seated on this seat?

Uttering the Adya Vija, and then saying "this water is for washing the feet of the (Adya). To the Devata Namah," offer the water at the feet of the Devi. Similarly with the word Svaha, in place of Namah, the offering should be placed at the head of the Devi. Then the wise worshipper with Svadha should offer the water for rinsing the mouth to the mouth of the Devi, and then the worshipper should offer to the lotus-mouth of the Devi Madhu-parka with the Mantra Svadha. He should then offer water to rinse the mouth (a second time) with the Mantra "Vang Svadha". Then the worshipper, saying:

Mantra

Hring, Shring, Kring, Parameshvari, Svaha: I offer this water for bathing, this apparel, these jewels, to the Supreme Devi, the Primordial Kalika. Svaha, make an offer of them to all parts of the body of the Devi.

Then the worshipper should, with the same Mantra, but ending with Namah, offer scent with his middle and third finger to the heart-lotus (of the Devi), and with the same Mantra, but ending with Vaushat, he should similarly offer to Her flowers. Having placed the burning incense and lighted lamp in front of Devi, and sprinkling them with water, they should be given away with the

Mantra

Hring, Shring, Kring, Parameshvari, Svaha: This incense-stick and light I humbly offer to Adya-Kalika. Svaha.

After worship of the Bell with the

Mantra

O Mother, Who produces the sound which proclaims triumph to Thee. Svaha, he should ring it with his left hand, and, taking up the incense-stick with his right hand, he should wave it up to the nostrils of the Devi. Then, placing the incense-stick on Her left, he should raise and wave the light ten times up to and before the eyes of the Devi. Then, taking the Cup and the Shuddhi in his two hands, the worshipper should, whilst uttering the Mula-Mantra, offer them to the centre of the Yantra.

Mantra

O Thou who hast brought to an end a crore of kalpas, take this excellent wine, as also the Shuddhi, and grant to me endless liberation.

Then, drawing a figure (in front of the Yantra), according to the rules of ordinary worship, place the plate with food thereon. Sprinkle the food (with the Mantra Phat) and veil it with the Avagunthana-Mudra (and the Mantra Hung), and then again protect it (by the Mantra Phat) (Saying Vang), and, exhibiting the Dhenu-Mudra over it, make it into the food of immortality. Then, after recitation of the Mula-Mantra seven times, it should be offered to the Devi with the water taken from the vessel of offering.

The worshipper, after reciting the Mula-Mantra, should say: "This cooked food, with all other necessaries, I offer to the Adya-Kali, my Ishta-devi." He should then say: "O Shiva! partake of this offering". Then he should make the Devi eat the offering by means of the five Mudras called Prana, Apana, Samana, Vyana, and Udana.

Next, form with the left hand the Naivedya-Mudra, which is like a full-blown lotus. Then, whilst reciting the Mula-Mantra, give away the jar with wine to the Devi for Her to drink. After that offer again water for rinsing the mouth, and following that a threefold oblation should be made to the Devi with wine from the cup of the Shri-patra. Then, reciting the Mula-Mantra, let the worshipper offer five handfuls of flowers to the head, heart, Muladhara Lotus, the feet, and all parts of the body of the Devi, and thereafter with folded palms he should pray to his Ishta-devata thus:

Mantra

O Ishta-devata! I am now worshipping the Devatas who surround thee, namah.

The six parts of the body of the Devi should then be worshipped at the four corners of the Yantra, and in front and behind it in their order; and then the line of Gurus should be worshipped. Then, with scent and flowers, worship the four Kula-gurus – namely, Guru, Parama-guru, Parapara-guru, Parameshti-guru.

Then, with the wine in the cup of the Guru, make three Tarpanas to each, and on the lotus of eight petals worship the eight Mother Nayikas – namely, Mangala, Vijaya, Bhadra, Jayanti, Aparajita, Nandini, Narasinghi, and Kaumari (99-100), and on the tips of the petals worship the eight Bhairavas – Asitanga, Ruru, Chanda, Krodhonmatta, Bhayangkara, Kapali, Bhishana, and Sanghara. Indra and the other Dik-palas should be worshipped in the Bhu-pura, and their weapons outside the Bhu-pura, and then Tarpana should be made to them.

After worshipping (the Devi) with all the offerings, sacrifice should be carefully made to Her. The ten approved beasts which may be sacrificed are – deer, goat, sheep, buffalo, hog, porcupine, hare, iguana, and rhinoceros; but other beasts may also be sacrificed if the worshipper so desires. The worshipper versed in the rules of sacrifice should select a beast with good signs, and, placing it before the Devi, should sprinkle it with the water from the Vishesharghya, and by the Dhenu-Mudra should make it into nectar.

Let him then worship the goat (sheep, or whatever other animal is being sacrificed) with (the Mantra) "Namah to the goat," which is a beast, and with perfumes, flowers, vermilion, food, and water. Then he should whisper into the ears of the beast the Gayatri Mantra, which severs the bond of its life as a beast. The Pashu-Gayatri, which liberates a beast from its life of a beast, is as follows: After the word "Pashu-pashaya" say " Vidmahe," then, after the word "Vishva-karmane," say "Dhimahi," and then "Tanno jivah prachodayat."

Mantra

Let us bring to mind the bonds of the life of a beast. Let us meditate upon the Creator of the Universe. May He liberate us from out of this life (of a beast).

Then, taking the sacrificial knife, the excellent worshipper should worship it with the Vija "Hung," and worship Sarasvati and Brahma at its end, Lakshmi and Narayana at its middle, and Uma and Maheshvara at the handle. Then the sacrificial knife should be worshipped with the

Mantra

Namah to the sacrificial knife infused with the presence of Brahma, Vishnu, Shiva, and their Shaktis.

Then, dedicating it with the Great Word, he should, with folded hands, say: "May this dedication to Thee be according to the ordained rites".

Having thus offered the beast to the Devi, it should be placed on the ground. The worshipper then, with mind intent upon the Devi, should sever the head of the beast with one sharp stroke. This may be done either by the worshipper himself or by his brother, brother's son, a friend, or a kinsman, but never by one who is an enemy. The blood, when yet warm, should be offered to the Vatukas. Then the head with a light on it should be offered to the Devi with the following:

Mantra

"This head with the light upon it I offer to the Devi with obeisance ".

This is the sacrificial rite of the Kaulikas in Kaula worship. If it be not observed, the Devata is never pleased. After this Homa should be performed. Listen, O Beloved One! to the rules which relate to it. The worshipper should, with sand, make on his right a square, each side of which is one cubit. Let him, then, while reciting the Mula-Mantra, gaze at it, stroke it with a wisp of kusha grass, uttering the Weapon-Vija, and then sprinkle it with water to the accompaniment of the same Vija.

Then, veiling it with the Kurchcha-Vija, he should say: "Obeisance to the sthandila of the Devi," and with this Mantra worship the square. Then, inside the square three lines should be drawn from East to West, and three lines from South to North, of the length of a pradesha. When this has been done, the (following Devatas, whose names are hereinafter given) should be worshipped over these lines. Over the lines from West to East worship Mukunda, Isha, and Purandara: over the lines from South to North, Brahma, Vaivasvata, and Indu.

Mantra

Rang, Salutation to the seat of Fire.

Then the Mantrin should meditate upon the Devi Sarasvati after She has bathed, with eyes like the blue lotus on the seat of Fire in the embrace of Vagishvara, and worship in the seat of Fire with the Maya-Vija.

Then let him bring Fire in the manner prescribed, and gaze intently on it, and, whilst repeating the Mula-Mantra, invoke Vahni into it with the Mantra Phat. Then the seat of Fire should be worshipped in the Yantra with the

Mantra

Ong Salutation to the Yoga-pitha of Fire, and on the four sides, beginning on the East and ending on the South, Vama, Jyeshtha, Raudri, Ambika, should be worshipped in the order given.

Then the marked-off space should be worshipped with the

Mantra

Salutation to the sthandila of the revered Devata, the Primeval Kalika: and then within this place the worshipper should meditate upon the Devi Vagishvari under the form of the Mula-Devata. After lighting the Fire with the Vija Rang, and reciting the Mula-Mantra, and then the

Mantra

Hung Phat: to the eaters of raw flesh: Svaha, the share of the raw meat eaters (Rakshasas) should be put aside. Gaze at the Fire, saying the Weapon-Mantra, and surround it with the Veil Mudra, uttering the Vija Hung. Make the Fire into nectar with the Dhenu-Mudra. Take some Fire in both palms, and wave it thrice in a circle over the sthandila from right to left. Then with both knees on the ground, and meditating on Fire as the male seed of Shiva, the worshipper should place it into that portion of the Yoni Yantra which is nearest him. Then, first, worship the Image of Fire with the

Mantra

Hring, Salutation to the Image of Fire, and after that the Spirit of Fire with the

Mantra

Rang: to the Spirit of Fire namah.

The Mantrin will then think in his mind of the awakened form of Vahni, and kindle the fire with the following

Mantra

Ong, yellow Spirit of Fire, which knows all, destroy, destroy, burn, burn, ripen, ripen command: Svaha.

This is the Mantra for kindling Fire. After this, with folded hands, Fire should again be adored.

Mantra

I adore the kindled Fire of the colour of gold, free from impurity, burning, author of the Veda the devourer of oblations, which faces every quarter.

After adoration of Fire in this manner, cover the marked-off space with kusha grass, and then the worshipper, giving Fire the name of his own, Ishta-devata, should worship him.

Mantra

Ong,O Red-eyed One! Vaishvanara, origin of the Veda, come here, come, come here, (help me to) accomplish all (my) works: Svaha.

Then the seven Tongues of Fire, Hiranya and others, should be worshipped. The worshipper should next adore the six Limbs of Vahni uttering the word "of a thousand rays" in the dative singular, and at the end "obeisance to the heart".

Then the wise one should worship the forms of Vahni, the eight forms Jata-veda and others, and then the eight Shaktis – namely, Brahmi and others, the eight Nidhis – namely, Padma and others, and the ten Dik-palas – namely, Indra and others.

After worshipping the thunderbolt and other weapons, the sacrificer should take two blades of kusha grass of the length of the space between his stretched-out thumb and forefinger, and place them lengthwise in the ghee. He should meditate on the Nadi Ida in the left part of the ghee, and on the Nadi Pingala in the right portion, and on the Nadi Sushumna in the centre, and with a well-controlled mind take ghee from the right side, and offer it to the right eye of Vahni with the following:

Mantra

Ong to Agni Svaha.

Then, taking ghee from the left side, offer it to the left eye of Vahni with the

Mantra

Ong to Soma Svaha.

Then, taking ghee from the middle portion, offer it to the forehead of Vahni with the

Mantra

Ong to Agni and Soma Svaha.

Then, saying namah, take the ghee again from the right side, say first the Pranava, and then

Mantra

To Agni the Svishti-krit Svaha.

With this Mantra he should offer oblation to the mouth of Vahni. Then, uttering the Vyahriti with the Pranava at the commencement, and Svaha at the end, the Homa sacrifice should be performed. Then he should offer oblations thrice with the

Mantra

Om,O Vaishvanara, origin of the Veda, come hither, come hither, O Red-eyed One! and fulfil all my works

Then, invoking the Ishta-Devata with the proper Mantra into the Fire, let him worship Her and the Pitha-Devata. Twenty-five oblations should then be offered (uttering the Mula-Mantra with Svaha at the end), and, contemplating on the union (or identity) of his own soul with Vahni and the Devi, eleven oblations should also be offered with the Mula-Mantra to the Anga-Devatas, concluding with Svaha.

Then, with a mixture of ghee, tila-seed, honey, or with flowers and bael-leaves, or with (other prescribed) articles, oblation should be made for the attainment of one's desire. This oblation should be made not less than eight times, and with every attention and care. Then, reciting the primary Mantra ending with Svaha, complete oblation should be made (with a full ladle) with fruits and leaves. The worshipper, with the Sanghara-Mudra, transferring the Devi from the Fire to the lotus of his heart, should then say "Pardon me," and dismiss Him who feeds on oblations. Then, distributing presents, the Mantrin should consider that the Homa has been duly performed.

Then the excellent worshipper should place between the eyebrows what is left over of the oblations. This is the ordinance relating to Homa in all forms of Agama worship. After performance of Homa the worshipper should proceed to do japa. Now, listen,O Devi! to the instructions which relate to japa by which the Vidya is pleased. During japa, the Devata, the Guru, and the Mantra should be considered as one. The letters of the Mantra are the Devata, and the Devata is in the form of the Guru. To him who worships them as one and the same, his is the greatest success.

The worshipper should then meditate upon his Guru as being in his head, the Devi in his heart, the Mula-Mantra in the form of tejas on his tongue, and himself as united with the glory of all three. Then, adding the Tara to the beginning and the end of the Mula-Mantra, it should be made japa of seven times, and then it should be recapitulated with the Matrika Vija at its beginning and end. The wise worshipper should make japa of the Maya-Vija over his head ten times, and of the Pranava ten times over his mouth, and of the Maya-Vija again seven times in the lotus of his heart, and then perform Pranayama.

Then, taking a rosary of coral, etc, let him worship it thus:

Mantra

O rosary,O rosary,O great rosary, thou art the image of all Shaktis. Thou art the repository of the fourfold blessings. Do thou therefore be the giver to me of all success.

Having thus worshipped the Mala, and also made Tarpana to it thrice with wine taken from the Shri-patra, accompanied by recitation of the Mula-Mantra, the worshipper should, with well-controlled mind, make japa one thousand and eight, or at least one hundred and eight times. Then, doing Pranayama, he should offer on the left lotus-hand of the Devi the fruit of his japa, whose form is Tejas, together with water and flowers from the Shri-patra, and, bowing down his head to the ground, say the following:

Mantra

O Great Queen! Thou Who protectest that which is most secret, deign to accept this my recitation. May by Thy grace success attend my effort.

After this, let him with folded hands recite the hymn and the protective Mantra. Then the Sadhaka should, with the special oblation in his hand, going round the Devi, keeping Her to his right, say the following, and dedicate his own self by offering Vilomarghya.

Mantra

Om, whatsoever ere this I in the possession of life, intelligence, body, or in action, awake, in dream or dreamless sleep have done, whether by word or deed, by my hands, feet, belly, or organ of generation, whatsoever I have remembered or spoken – of all that I make an offering to Brahman. I and all that is mine I lay at the lotus-feet of the Adya Kali. I make the sacrifice of myself Ong tat sat.

Then, with folded hands, let him supplicate his Ishta-Devata, and reciting the Maya-Mantra, say:

Mantra

"O Primordial Kalika! I have worshipped Thee with all my powers and devotion," and then saying, "Forgive me," let him bid the Devi go. Let him with his hands formed into Sanghara-Mudra take up a flower, smell it, and place it on his heart. A triangular figure well and clearly made should next be drawn in the North-East corner, and there he should worship the Devi Nirmalya-vasini with the

Mantra

Hring salutation to the Devi Nirmalya-vasini.

Then, distributing Naivedya to Brahma, Vishnu, and Shiva, and all the other Devas, the worshipper should partake of it. Then, placing his Shakti on a separate seat to his left, or on the same seat with himself, he should make a pleasing drink in the cup, The cup should be so formed as to hold not more than five and not less than three tolas of wine, and may be of either gold or silver, or crystal, or made of the shell of a cocoa-nut. It should be kept on a support on the right side of the plate containing the prepared food.

Then the wise one should serve the sacred food and wine either himself or by his brother's sons among the worshippers according to the order of their seniority. The purified wine should be served in the drinking-cups, and the purified food in plates kept for that purpose, and then should food and drink be taken with such as are present at the time. First of all, some purified food should be eaten to make a bed as it were (for the wine which is to be drunk). Let the assembled worshippers then joyously take up each his own cup filled with excellent nectar.

Then let him take up each his own cup and meditate upon the Kula-Kundalini, who is the Chit, and who is spread from the Muladhara lotus to the tip of the tongue, and, uttering the Mula-Mantra, let each, after taking the others' permission, offer it as oblation to the mouth of the Kundali. When the Shakti is of the household, the smelling of the wine is the equivalent of drinking it. Worshippers who are householders may drink five cups only. Excessive drinking prevents the attainment of success by Kula worshippers.

They may drink until the sight or the mind is not affected. To drink beyond that is bestial. How is it possible for a sinner who becomes a fool through drink and who shows contempt for the Sadhaka of Shakti to say "I worship the Adya Kalika"?. As touch cannot affect food, etc, offered to Brahman, so there is no distinction of caste in food offered to Thee.

As I have directed, so should eating and drinking be done. After partaking of food offeredto Thee, the hands should not be washed, but with a piece of cloth or a little water remove that which has adhered to the hands. Lastly, after placing a flower from the nirmalya on his head, and wearing a tilaka mark made from the remnants of the oblation on the Yantra between his eyebrows, the intelligent worshipper may roam the earth like a Deva.

End of the Sixth Joyful Message, entitled "Placing of the Shri-patra, Homa, Formation of the Chakra, and other Rites."

Chapter 7

Hymn of Praise (Stotra), Amulet (Kavacha), and the description of the Kula-tattva

PARVATI was pleased at hearing the revelation of the auspicious Mantra of the Adya Kalika, which yields abundant blessings, is the only means of attaining to a knowledge of the Divine essence, and leads to liberation; as also at hearing of the morning rites, the rules relating to bathing, Sandhya, the purification of Bhang, the methods of external and internal Nyasa and worship, the sacrifice of animals, Homa, the formation of the circle of worship, and the partaking of the holy food. Bowing low with modesty, the Devi questioned Shankara.

Shri Devi said:

O Sadashiva! Lord, and Benefactor of the Universe, Thou hast in Thy mercy spoken of the mode of worship of the supreme Prakriti, which benefits all being, is the sole path both for enjoyment and final liberation, and which gives, in this Age, in particular, immediate success. My mind, immersed in the ocean of the nectar of Thy word, has no desire to rise therefrom, but craves for more and more. O Deva, in the directions Thou hast given relating to the worship of the great Devi, Thou hast but given a glimpse of the hymn of praise, and of the protective Mantra. Do Thou reveal them now.

Shri Sadashiva said:

Listen, then, O Devi, Who art the adored of the worlds,to this unsurpassed hymn, by the reciting of or listening to which one becomes the Lord of all the Siddhis, (a hymn) which allays evil fortune, increases happiness and prosperity, destroys untimely death, and removes all calamities, and is the cause of the happy approach to the gracious Adya Kalika. It is by the grace of this hymn,O Happy One, that I am Tripurari.

O Devi! the Rishi of this hymn is Sadashiva, its metre is Anushtup, its Devata is the Adya Kalika, and the object of its use is the attainment of Dharmma, Artha, Kama, and Moksha.

64

Hymn Entitled Adya-Kali-Svarupa.

Hring, O Destroyer of Time,
Shring, O Terrific One,
Kring, Thou Who art beneficent,
Possessor of all the Arts,
Thou art Kamala,
Destroyer of the pride of the Kali Age,
Who art kind to Him of the matted hair,
Devourer of Him Who devours,
Mother of Time,
Thou Who art brilliant as the Fires of the final Dissolution,
Wife of Him of the matted hair,
O Thou of formidable countenance,
Ocean of the nectar of compassion,
Merciful,
Vessel of Mercy,
Whose Mercy is without limit,
Who art attainable alone by Thy mercy,
Who art Fire,
Tawny,
Black of hue,
Thou Who increasest the joy of the Lord of Creation,
Night of Darkness,
Image of Desire,
Yet Liberator from the bonds of desire,
Thou Who art (dark) as a bank of Clouds,
And bearest the crescent-moon,
Destructress of sin in the Kali Age,
Thou Who art pleased by the worship of virgins,
Thou Who art the Refuge of the worshippers of virgins,
Who art pleased by the feasting of the virgins,
Who art the Image of the virgin,
Thou Who wanderest in the kadamba forest,
Who art pleased with the flowers of the kadamba forest,
Who hast Thy abode in the kadamba forest,
Who wearest a garland of kadamba flowers,
Thou Who art youthful,
Who hast a soft low voice,
Whose voice is sweet as the cry of a Chakravaka bird,
Who drinkest and art pleased with the kadambari wine,
And Whose cup is a skull,
Who wearest a garland of bones,
Who art pleased with,
And Who art seated on the Lotus,
Who abidest in the centre of the Lotus,

65

Whom the fragrance of the Lotus pleases,
Who movest with the swaying gait of a Hangsa,
Destroyer of fear,
Who assumest all forms at will,
Whose abode is at Kama-rupa,
Who ever plays at the Kama-pitha,
O beautiful One,
O Creeper Which givest every desire,
Who art the Possessor of beautiful ornaments,
Adorable as the Image of all tenderness,
Thou with a tender body,
And Who art slender of waist,
Who art pleased with the nectar of purified wine,
Giver of success to them whom purified wine rejoices,
The own Deity of those who worship Thee when joyed with wine,
Who art gladdened by the worship of Thyself with purified wine,
Who art immersed in the ocean of purified wine,
Who art the Protectress of those who accomplish vrata with wine,
Whom the fragrance of musk gladdens,
And Who art luminous with a tilaka-mark of musk,
Who art attached to those who worship Thee with musk,
Who lovest those who worship Thee with musk,
Who art a Mother to those who burn musk as incense,
Who art fond of the musk-deer and art pleased to eat its musk,
Whom the scent of camphor gladdens,
Who art adorned with garlands of camphor,
And Whose body is smeared with camphor and sandal paste,
Who art pleased with purified wine flavoured with Camphor,
Who drinkest purified wine flavoured with camphor,
Who art bathed in the ocean of camphor,
Whose abode is in the ocean of camphor,
Who art pleased when worshipped with the Vija Hung,
Thou Who threatenest with the Vija Hung,
Embodiment of Kulachara,
Adored by Kaulikas,
Benefactress of the Kaulikas,
Observant of Kulachara,
Joyous One, Revealer of the path of the Kaulikas,
Queen of Kashi,
Allayer of sufferings,
Giver of blessings to the Lord of Kashi,(28)
Giver of pleasure to the Lord of Kashi,
Beloved of the Lord of Kashi,
Thou Whose toe-ring bells make sweet melody as Thou movest,
Whose girdle bells sweetly tinkle,
Who abidest in the mountain of gold,
Who art like a Moon-beam on the mountain of gold,
Who art gladdened by the recitation of the Mantra Kling,
Who art the Kama Vija,
Destructress of all evil inclinations,

And of the afflictions of the Kaulikas,
Lady of the Kaulas,
O Thou Who by the three Vijas, Kring, Hring, Shring, art the
Destructress of the fear of Death.
(To Thee I make obeisance.)

These are proclaimed as the Hundred Names of Kalika, beginning with the letter Ka. They are all identical with the image of Kali. He who in worship recites these names with his mind fixed on Kalika, for him Mantra-siddhi is quickly obtained, and with him Kali is pleased. By the mere bidding of his Guru he acquires intelligence, knowledge, and becomes wealthy, famous, munificent, and compassionate. Such an one enjoys life happily in this world with his children and grandchildren with wealth and dominion. He who, on a new moon night, when it falls on Tuesday, worships the great Adya Kali, Mistress of the three worlds, with the five Ma-karas, and repeats Her hundred names, becomes suffused with the presence of the Devi, and for him there remains nothing in the three worlds which is beyond his powers.

He becomes in learning like Brihaspati himself, in wealth like Kuvera. His profundity is that of the ocean, and his strength that of the wind. He shines with the blinding brilliance of the Sun, yet pleases with the soft glamour of the Moon. In beauty he becomes like the God of Love, and reaches the hearts of women. He comes forth as conqueror everywhere by the grace of this hymn of praise. Singing this hymn, he attains all his desires. All these desires he shall attain by the grace of the gracious Adya, whether in battle, in seeking the favour of Kings, in wagers, or in disputes, and when his life be in danger, at the hands of robbers, amidst burning villages, lions, or tigers, in forests and lonely deserts, when imprisoned, threatened by Kings or adverse planets, in burning fever, in long sickness, when attacked by fearful disease, in the sickness of children caused by the influence of adverse planets, or when tormented by evil dreams, when fallen in boundless waters, and when he be in some storm-tossed ship.

O Devi! he who with firm devotion meditates upon the Parama Maya— image of the most excellent Kali—is without a doubt relieved of all dangers. For him there is never any fear, whether arising from sin or disease. For him there is ever victory, and defeat never. At the mere sight of him all dangers flee. He expounds all Scriptures, enjoys all good fortune, and becomes the leader in all matters of caste and duty, and the lord among his kinsmen. In his mouth Vani ever abides, and in his home Kamala. Men bow with respect at the mere mention of his name. The eight Siddhis, such as Anima and others, he looks upon as but mere bits of grass.

I have now recited the hymn of a hundred names, which is called "The Very Form of the Adya Kali".

Purashcharana of this hymn, which is its repetition one hundred and eight times, yields all desired fruit. This hymn of praise of a hundred names, which is the Primeval Kali Herself, if read, or caused to be read, if heard, or caused to be heard, frees from all sins and leads to union with Brahman.

Shri Sadashiva said.

I have spoken of the great hymn of the Prakriti of the Supreme Brahman, hear now the protective Mantra of the sacred Adya Kalika. The name of the Mantra is "Conqueror of the three Worlds," its Rishi is Shiva, the verse is Anushtup, and its Devata the Adya Kali.

Its Vija is the Maya Vija, its Shakti is Kama Vija, and its Kilaka is Kring. It should be used for the attainment of all desired objects.

The Protective Mantra

(Known As Trailokya-Vijaya)

Hring, may the Adya protect my head;
Shring, may Kali protect my face;
Kring, may the Supreme Shakti protect my heart;
May She Who is the Supreme of the Supreme protect my throat;
May Jagaddhatri protect my two eyes;
May Shankari protect my two ears;
May Mahamaya protect my power of smell;
May Sarvva-mangala protect my taste;
May Kaumari protect my teeth;
May Kamalalaya protect my cheeks;
May Kshama protect my upper and lower lips;
May Charu-hasini protect my chin;
May Kuleshani protect my neck;
May Kripa-mayi protect the nape of my neck;
May Bahu-da protect my two arms;
May Kaivalya-dayini protect my two hands;
May Kapardini protect my shoulders;
May Trailokya-tarini protect my back;
May Aparna protect my two sides;
May Kamathasana protect my hips;
May Vishalakshi protect my navel;
May Prabha-vati protect my organ of generation;
May Kalyani protect my thighs;
May Parvati protect my feet;
May Jaya-durga protect my vital breaths,
And Sarvva-siddhi-da protect all parts of my body.

As to those parts as have not been mentioned in the Kavacha, and are unprotected, may the Eternal Primeval Kali protect all such.

I have now spoken to Thee of the wonderful heavenly Protective Mantra of the Adya Devi Kalika, which is known as the "Conqueror of the three Worlds".

He who repeats it at his devotions with his mind fixed upon the Adya obtains all his desires, and She becomes propitious unto him. He quickly attains Mantra-siddhi. The lesser siddhis become, as it were, his slaves. He who is childless gets a son, he who desires wealth gains riches. The seeker of learning attains it, and whatsoever a man desires he attains the same.

The Purashcharana of this Protective Mantra is its repetition a thousand times, and this gives the desired fruit. If it be written on birch-bark, with the paste of sandal, fragrant aloe, musk, saffron, or red sandal, and encased in a golden ball, worn either on the right arm, round the neck, in the crown lock, or round the waist, then the Adya Kali becomes devoted to its wearer, and grants him whatsoever he may desire. Nowhere has he fear. In all places he is a conqueror. He becomes ready of speech, free from ailments, long-lived and strong, endowed with all power of endurance, and an adept in all learning. He knows the meaning of all Scriptures, has Kings under his control, and holds both pleasure and emancipation in the hollow of his hand.

For men affected with the taint of the Kali Age it is a most excellent Mantra for the attainment of final liberation.

Shri Devi said:

Thou hast, O Lord! in Thy kindness told me of the Hymn and Protective Mantra; I now desire to hear of the rules relating to Purashcharana.

Shri Sadashiva said:

The rules relating to Purashcharana in the worship of the Adya Kalika are the same as those relating to the Purashcharana in the worship with the Brahma-Mantra. For Sadhakas who are unable to do them completely, both Japa, Puja and Homa, and Purashcharana may be curtailed, since it is better to observe these rites on a small scale than not to observe them at all. Now listen, O Gentle One! the while I describe to Thee the shortened form of worship. Let the wise one rinse his mouth with the Mula-Mantra, and then perform Rishi-nyasa. Let him purify the palms of the hands, and proceed to Kara-nyasa and Anga-nyasa. Passing the hands all over the body, let him practise Pranayama, and then meditate, worship, and inwardly recite. This is the ceremonial for the shortened form of worship.

In this form of worship, in lieu of Homa and other rites, the Mantras may be recited four times the number prescribed in the case of each of them respectively. There is also another mode of performance. A person who, when the fourteenth day of the dark half of the month falls on a Tuesday or Saturday, worships Jaganmayi with the five elements of worship, and recites with fully attentive mind the Mantra ten thousand times at midnight and feasts believers in the Brahman has performed Purashcharana. From one Tuesday to another Tuesday the Mantra should every day be inwardly recited a thousand times. The Mantra thus recited eight thousand times is equal to the performance of Purashcharana.

In all Ages, O Devi! but particularly in the Kali Age, the Mantras of the Sacred Primeval Kalika are of great efficacy, and yield complete success. O Parvati! In the Kali Age, Kali in her various forms is ever watchful, but when the Kali Age is in full sway, then the form of Kali Herself is for the benefit of the world. In initiation into this Kalika Mantra there is no necessity to determine whether it be siddha or su-siddha, or the like, or favourable or inimical. If japa is made of it, which is both niyama and a-niyama, the Adya Devi is pleased. The mortal, by the grace of the glorious Adya, attains a knowledge of the divine essence, and, possessed of such knowledge, is, without a doubt, liberated even while living. Beloved, there is no need here for over-exertion or endurance or penances. The religious exercises of the worshippers of the Adya Kali are pleasant to accomplish. By the mere purification of the heart the worshipper attains all that he desires. So long, however, as the heart is not purified, so long must the worshipper practise the rites with devotion to Kula.

The carrying out of the practices ordained produces purification of the heart. The Mantra should, however, first be received from the mouth of the Guru in the case of the Brahma-Mantra. O Great Queen! Purashkriya should be done after the performance of the necessary worship and of other prescribed rites. In the purified heart knowledge of Brahman grows. And when knowledge of Brahman is attained, there is neither that which should, nor that which should not, be done.

Shri Parvati said:

O Great Deva! what is Kula, and what is Kulachara? O Great Lord! what is the sign of each of the five elements of worship? I desire to hear the truth relating to these.

Shri Sadashiva said:

Thou hast asked well, O Lady of the Kulas. Thou art indeed the Benefactress of the worshippers. Listen! For Thy pleasure I shall accurately describe to Thee these things. The Kula are Jiva, Prakriti, space, time, ether, earth, water, fire, and air. O Primeval One! the realization that all this is one with Brahman is Kulachara, and produces Dharmma, Artha, Kama, and Moksha. Those whose sins are washed away by merits acquired in various previous births by penances, alms, and faithful observance of worship, it is they whose minds are inclined in Kaulika worship. When the intelligence realizes the essence of Kaulika worship, it becomes at once purified, and the mind inclines to the lotus-feet of the Primeval Kali. The excellent worshipper versed in Kaula doctrine who has received this most excellent Vidya by the service of a good spiritual teacher, if he remains firmly attached to Kaulika worship and to the worship with the five elements of the Primeval Kalika, the Patron Devi of Kula, will enjoy a multitude of blessings in this life, and attain final liberation at its close.

The characteristic of the first element is that it is the great medicine for humanity, helping it to forget deep sorrows, and is the cause of joy. But, O Dearest One! the element which is not purified stupefies and bewilders, breeds disputes and diseases, and should be rejected by the Kaulas. Beasts bred in villages, in the air, or forest, which are nourishing, and increase intelligence, energy, and strength, are the second element. O Beautiful One! of the animals bred in water, that which is pleasing and of good taste, and increases the generative power of man, is the third element. The characteristics of the fourth element are that it is easily obtainable, grown in the earth, and is the root of the life of the three worlds. And, O Devi, the signs of the fifth element are that it is the cause of intense pleasure to all living things, is the origin of all creatures, and the root of the world which is without either beginning or end. Know, Dearest One! that the first element is fire, the second is air, the third is water, the fourth is the earth, and, O Beauteous Face! as to the fifth element, know it to be ether, the support of the Universe. O Sovereign Mistress of Kula, he who knows Kula, the five Kula-tattvas, and Kula worship, is liberated whilst yet living.

End of the Seventh Joyful Message, entitled "Hymn of Praise (Stotra), Amulet (Kavacha), and the description of the Kula-tattva."

Chapter 8

The Dharmma and Customs of the Castes and Ashramas

AFTER hearing of the various forms of Dharmma, Bhavani, Mother of the worlds, Destructress of all worldly bonds, spoke again to Shankara.

Shri Devi said:

I have heard of the different Dharmma, which bring happiness in this world and the next, and bestow piety, wealth, fulfilment of desire, ward off danger, and are the cause of union with the Supreme. I wish now to hear of the castes and of the stages of life. Speak in Thy kindness, O Omnipresent One! of these, and of the mode of life which should be observed therein.

Shri Sadashiva said:

O Thou of auspicious Vows! in the Satya and other Ages there were four castes; in each of these were four stages of life, and the rules of conduct varied according to the caste and stages of life. In the Kali Age, however, there are five castes–namely, Brahmana, Kshatriya, Vaishya, Shudra, and Samanya. Each of these five castes, O Great Queen! have two stages of life. Listen, then, Adye! whilst I narrate to Thee their mode of life, rites, and duties. I have already spoken to Thee of the incapacity of men born in the Kali Age. Unused as they are to penance, and devoid of learning in the Vedas, short-lived, and incapable of strenuous effort, how can they endure bodily labour?.

O Beloved! there is in the Kali Age no Brahmacharya nor Vanaprastha. There are two stages only, Grihastha and Bhikshuka. O Auspicious One! In the Kali Age the householder should in all his acts be guided by the rules of the Agamas. He will never attain success by other ways. And, O Devi! at the stage of the mendicant the carrying of the staff is not permitted, since, O Thou of Divine Knowledge! both that and other practices are Vedic. In the Kali Age, O Gentle One! the adoption of the life of an Avadhuta, according to the Shaiva rites, is in the Kali Age equivalent to the entry into the life of a Sannyasin. When the Kali Age is in full sway, the Vipras and the other castes have equal right to enter into both these stages of life The purificatory rites of all are to be according to the rules ordained by Shiva, though the particular practices of the Vipras and other castes vary.

A man becomes a householder the moment he is born. It is by Sangskara that he enters upon any of the other stages of life. For this reason, O Great Queen! One should first be a householder, following the rules of that mode of life. When, however, one is freed of worldly desires by the knowledge of the Real, it is then that one should abandon all and seek refuge in the life of an ascetic. In childhood one should acquire knowledge; in youth, wealth and wife. The wise man in middle age will devote himself to acts of religion, and in his old age he should retire from the world.

No one should retire from the world who has an old father or mother, a devoted and chaste wife, or young and helpless children. He who becomes an ascetic, leaving mothers, fathers, infant children, wives, agnates and cognates, is guilty of a great sin. He who becomes a mendicant without first satisfying the need of his own parents and relatives is guilty of the sins of killing his father and mother, a woman, and a Brahmana. The Brahmanas and men of other castes should perform their respective purificatory rites according to the ordinances laid down by Shiva. This is the rule in the Kali Age.

Shri Devi said:

O Omnipresent One! tell Me what is the rule of life for the householder and mendicant, and what are the purificatory rites for the Vipras and other castes.

Shri Sadashiva said:

The state of an householder is for all the descendants of Manu the first duty. I shall, therefore, first speak of it, and do Thou listen to Me, O Lady of the Kaulas. A householder should be devoted to the contemplation of Brahman and possessed of the knowledge of Brahman, and should consign whatever he does to Brahman. He should not tell an untruth, or practise deceit, and should ever be engaged in the worship of the Devatas and guests. Regarding his father and mother as two visible incarnate deities, he should ever and by every means in his power serve them. O Shiva! O Parvati! if the mother and father are pleased, Thou too art pleased. and the Supreme Being is propitious to him. O Primeval One! Thou art the Mother of the Worlds, and the Supreme Brahman is the Father; what better religious act can there be than that which pleases You both?. According to their requirements, one should offer seats, beds, clothes, drink, and food to mother and father. They should always be spoken to in a gentle voice, and their children's demeanour should ever be agreeable to them. The good son who ever obeys the behests of his mother and father hallows the family. If one desires one's own welfare, all arrogance, mockery, threats, and angry words should be avoided in the parents' presence. The son who is

73

obedient to his parents should, out of reverence to them, bow to them and stand up when he sees them, and should not take his seat without their permission. He who, intoxicated with the pride of learning or wealth, slights his parents, is beyond the pale of all Dharmma, and goes to a terrible Hell. Even if the vital breath were to reach his throat, the householder should not eat without first feeding his mother, father, son, wife, guest, and brother. The man who, to the deprivation of his elders and equals, fills his own belly is despised in this world, and goes to Hell in the next. The householder should cherish his wife, educate his children, and support his kinsmen and friends. This is the supreme eternal duty. The body is nourished by the mother. It originates from the father. The kinsmen, out of love, teach. The man, therefore, who forsakes them is indeed vile. For their sake should an hundred pains be undergone. With all one's ability they should be pleased. This is the eternal duty. That man who in this world turns his mind to Brahman and adheres faithfully to the truth is above all a man of good deeds, and knows the Supreme, and is blest in all the worlds. The householder should never punish his wife, but should cherish her like a mother. If she is virtuous and devoted to her husband, he should never forsake her even in times of greatest misfortune. The wise man, whilst his own wife is living, should never with wicked intent touch another woman, otherwise he will go to hell. The wise man should not, when in a private place, live and sleep or lie down close to other men's wives. He should avoid all improper speech and braggart boldness in their presence. By riches, clothes, love, respect, and pleasing words should one's wife be satisfied. The husband should never do anything displeasing to her. The wise man should not send his wife to any festival, concourse of people, pilgrimage, or to another's house, except she be attended by his son or an inmate of his own house.

O Maheshvari! that man whose wife is both faithful and happy is surely looked upon as if he had performed all Dharmma, and is truly Thy favourite also. A father should fondle and nurture his sons until their fourth year, and then until their sixteenth they should be taught learning and their duties. Up to their twentieth year they should be kept engaged in household duties, and thenceforward, considering them as equals, he should ever show affection towards them. In the same manner a daughter should be cherished and educated with great care, and then given away with money and jewels to a wise husband.

The householder should thus also cherish and protect his brothers and sisters and their children, his kinsmen, friends, and servants. He should also maintain his fellow-worshippers, fellow-villagers, and guests, whether ascetics or others. If the wealthy householder does not so act, then let him be known as a beast, a sinner, and one despised in the worlds. The householder should not be inordinately addicted to sleep, idling, care for the body, dressing his hair, eating or drinking, or attention to his clothes. He should be moderate as to food, sleep, speech, and sexual intercourse, and be sincere, humble, pure, free from sloth, and persevering. Chivalrous to his foes, modest before his friends, relatives, and elders, he should neither respect those who deserve censure nor slight those who are worthy of respect. Men should only be admitted to his trust and confidence after association with them and observation of their nature, inclination, conduct, and friendly character. Even an insignificant enemy should be feared, and one's own power should be disclosed only at the proper time. But on no account should one deviate from the path of duty. A religious man should not speak of his own fame and prowess, of what has been told him in secret, nor of the good that he has done for others. A man of good name should not engage in any quarrel with an unworthy motive, nor when defeat is certain, nor with those who are superior or inferior to himself He should diligently earn knowledge, wealth, fame, and religious merit, and avoid all vicious habits, the company of the wicked, falsehood, and treachery. Ventures should be undertaken according to the circumstances and one's condition in life, and actions should be done according to their season. Therefore, in everything that a man does he should first consider whether the circumstances and time are suitable. The householder should employ himself in the acquisition of what is necessary and in the protection of the same. He should be judicious, pious, good to his friends. He should be moderate in speech and laughter, in particular in the presence of those entitled to his reverence. He should hold his senses under control, be of cheerful disposition, think of what is good, be of firm resolve, attentive, far-sighted, and discriminating in the use of his senses.

The wise householder's speech should be truthful, mild, agreeable, and salutary, yet pleasing, avoiding both self-praise and the disparagement of others. The man who has dedicated tanks, planted trees, built rest-houses on the roadside, or bridges, has conquered the three worlds. That man who is the happiness of his mother and father, to whom his friends are devoted, and whose fame is sung by men, he is the conqueror of the three worlds. He whose aim is truth, whose charity is ever for the poor, who has mastered lust and anger, by him are the three worlds conquered. He who covets not others' wives or goods, who is free of deceit and envy, by him the three worlds are conquered. He who is not afraid in battle nor to go to war when there is need, and who dies in battle undertaken for a sacred cause, by him the three worlds are conquered. He whose soul is free from doubts, who is devoted to and a faithful follower of the ordinances of Shiva, and remains under My control, by him the three worlds are conquered. The wise man who in his conduct with his fellow-men looks with an equal eye upon friend and foe, by him are the three worlds conquered. O Devi! purity is of two kinds, external and internal. The dedication of oneself to Brahman is known as internal purity, and the cleansing of the impurities of the body by water or ashes, or any other matter which cleanses the body, is called external purity.

O Dearest One! the waters of Ganga, or of any other river, tank, pond, well, or pool, or of the celestial Ganga, are equally purifying. O Thou of auspicious Vows! the ashes from a place of sacrifice and cleansed earth are excellent, and the skin of an antelope and grass are as purifying as earth. O Auspicious One! what need is there to say more about purity and impurity? Whatever purifies the mind that the householder may do. Let there be external purification upon awakening from sleep, after sexual intercourse, making water, voiding the bowels, and at the close of a meal, and whenever dirt of any kind has been touched.

Sandhya, whether Vaidika or Tantrika should be performed thrice daily, and according as the worship changes so does its service. The worshippers of the Brahma-Mantra have performed their Sandhya when they have made japa of the Gayatri, realizing within themselves the identity of the Gayatri and Brahman. In the case of those who are not Brahma-worshippers, Vaidika Sandhya consists of the worship of and offering of oblations to the Sun and the recitation of the Gayatri.

O Gentle One! In all daily prayers recitation shouldbe done one thousand and eight or a hundred and eight or ten times. O Devi! the Shudras and Samanyas may observe any of the rites proclaimed by the Agamas, and by these they attain that which they desire. The three times of performance (of Sandhya) are at sunrise, at noon, and at sunset.

Shri Devi said:

Thou hast Thyself said, O Lord! that when the Kali Age is in full sway for all castes, commencing with the Brahmamas, Tantrika rites are alone appropriate. Why, then, dost Thou restrict the Vipras to Vedic rites? It behoveth Thee to explain this fully to Me.

Shri Sadashiva said:

O Thou Who knowest the essence of all things, truly hast Thou spoken. In the Kali Age all observances bear the fruit of enjoyment and liberation when done according to the rites of the Tantras. The Brahma-Savitri, though known as Vaidika, should be called Tantrika also, and is appropriate in both observances. It is, therefore, O Devi! that I have said that when the Kali Age is in full sway, the twice-born shall alone be entitled to the Gayatri, but not the other Mantras. In the Kali Age the Savitri should be said by the Brahmanas, preceded by the Tara, and by the Kshatriyas and Vaishyas, preceded by the Kamala and Vagbhava Vijas respectively. In order, O Supreme Devi! That a distinction may be drawn between the twice-born and the Shudras, the daily duties are directed to be preceded by Vaidika Sandhya. Success, however, may also be attained by the mere following of the ordinances of Shambhu. This is verily true, and I repeat it is true and very true, and there is no doubt about it. O Adored of the Devas! even if the stated time for the saying of the daily prayer is past, all who desire emancipation and are not prevented by sickness or weakness should say, "Ong the Ever-existent Brahman". The seat, clothes, vessels, bed, carriages, residence,

76

and household furniture of the worshipper should be as clean as possible. At the close of the daily prayers the householder should keep himself occupied with household duties or the study of the Vedas; he should never remain idle. In holy places, on holy days, or when the Sun or Moon is in eclipse, he should do inward recitation, and give alms, and thus become the abode of all that is good.

In the Kali Age life is dependent on the food that is eaten, fasting is therefore not recommended, in lieu of it, the giving of alms is ordained. O Great Queen! in the Kali Age alms are efficacious in the accomplishment of all things. The proper objects of such alms are the poor devoted to meritorious acts. O Mother! the first days of the month, of the year, of the lunar half-months, the fourteenth day of the lunar half-month, the eighth day of the light half of the lunar month, the eleventh day of the lunar half-month, the new moon, one's birthday, the anniversary of one's father's death, and days fixed as those of festivals, are holy days.

The River Ganges and all the great Rivers, the house of the religious Teacher, and the places of the Devas are holy places. But for those who, neglecting the study of the Veda, the service of mother and father, and the protection of their wife, go to places of pilgrimage, such holy places are changed to hell. For women there is no necessity to go on pilgrimage, to fast, or to do other like acts, nor is there any need to perform any devotion except that which consists in the service of their husband. For a woman her husband is a place of pilgrimage, the performance of penance, the giving of alms, the carrying out of vows, and her spiritual teacher. Therefore should a woman devote herself to the service of her husband with her whole self. She should ever by words and deeds of devotion act for the pleasure of her husband, and, remaining faithful to his behests, should please his relations and friends.

A woman whose husband is her vow should not look at him with hard eyes, or utter hard words before him. Not even in her thought should she do anything which is displeasing to her husband. She who by body, mind, and word, and by pleasant acts, ever pleases her husband, attains to the abode of Brahman. Remaining ever faithful to the wishes of her husband, she should not look upon the face of other men, or have converse with them, or uncover her body before them.

In childhood she should remain under the control of her parents, in her youth of her husband, and in her old age of the friends and relatives of her husband. She should never be independent.

A father should not marry his daughter if she does not know her duty to a husband and how to serve him, also the other rules of woman's conduct.

Neither the flesh of human beings, nor the animals resembling them, nor the flesh of the cow, which is serviceable in various ways, nor the flesh of carnivorous animals, nor such meat as is tasteless, should be eaten. Auspicious One! fruits and roots of various kinds whether grown in villages or jungles, and all that is grown in the ground, may be eaten at pleasure.

Teaching and the performance of sacrifices are the proper duties of a Brahmana. But if he be incapable of these, he may earn his livelihood by following the profession of a Kshatriya or Vaishya. The proper occupation of a Rajanya is that of fighting and ruling. But if he be incapable of these, he may earn his livelihood by following the profession of a Vaishya or Shudra. If a Vaishya cannot trade, then for him the following of the profession of a Shudra involves no blame. For a Shudra, O Sovereign Queen! service is the prescribed means of livelihood. O Devi! members of the Samanya class may for their maintenance follow all occupations except such as are specially reserved for the Brahmana. The latter, void of hate and attachment, self-controlled, truthful, the conqueror of his senses, free of envy and all guile, should pursue his own avocations. He should ever be the same to, and the well-wisher of, all men, and teach his well-behaved pupils as if they were his own sons. He should ever avoid falsehood, detraction, and vicious habits, arrogance, friendship for low persons, the pursuit of low objects, and the use of language which gives offence. Where peace is possible, avoid war. Peace with honour is excellent. O Adorable Face! for the Rajanya it should be either death or victory in battle. A man of the kingly caste should not covet the wealth of his subjects, or levy excessive taxes, but, being faithful to his promises, he should ever in the observance of his duty protect his subjects as though they were his own children. In government, war, treaties, and other affairs of State the King should take the advice of his Ministers. War should be carried on in accordance with Dharmma. Rewards and punishments should be awarded justly and in accordance with the Shastras. The best treaty should be concluded which his power allows. By stratagem should the end desired be attained. By the same means should wars be conducted and treaties concluded. Victory, peace, and prosperity follow stratagem. He should ever avoid the company of the low, and be good to the learned. He should be of a calm disposition judicious of action in time of trouble, of good conduct and reasonable in his expenditure.

He should be an expert in the maintenance of his forts, well trained in the use of arms. He should ever ascertain the disposition of his army, and teach his soldiers military tactics. O Devi! he should not in battle kill one who is stunned, who has surrendered his arms, or is a fugitive, nor those of his enemies whom he has capturedn nor their wives or children. Whatever is acquired either by victory or treaty should be distributed amongst the soldiers in shares according to merit.

The King should make known to himself the character and courage of each of his warriors, and if he would care for his interests he should not place a large army under the command of a single officer. He should not put his trust in any single person, nor place one man in charge of the administration, nor treat his inferiors as equals, nor be familiar with them. He should be very learned, yet not garrulous; full of knowledge, yet anxious to learn; full of honours, yet without arrogance. In awarding both reward and punishment he should be discriminating. The King should either himself or through his spies watch his subjects, kinsmen, and servants. A wise master should not either honour or degrade anyone in a fit of passion or arrogance and without due cause. Soldiers, commanders, ministers, wife, children, and servitors he should protect. If guilty, they should be punished according to their deserts. The King should protect, like a father, the insane, incapable, children and orphans, and those who are old and infirm. Know that agriculture and trade are the appropriate callings of the Vaishya. It is by agriculture and trade that man's body is maintained. Therefore, O Devi! in agriculture and trade all negligence, vicious habits, laziness, untruth, and deceit should be avoided with the whole soul. Shiva! when both buyer and seller are agreed as to the object of sale and the price thereof, and mutual promises have been made, then the purchase becomes complete. O Dearest One! the sale or gift of property by one who is a lunatic, out of his senses, under age, a captive, or enfeebled by disease, is invalid. The purchase of things not seen is concluded by hearing the description thereof. If the article be found to differ from its description, then the purchase is set aside. The sale of an elephant, a camel, and a horse is effected by the description of the animal. The sale is, however, set aside if the animal does not answer its description. If in the purchase of elephants, camels, and horses a latent vice becomes patent within the course of a year from the date of sale, then the purchase is set aside, but not after the lapse of one year. O Devi of the Kulas! the human body is the receptacle of piety, wealth, desires, and final liberation. It should therefore never be the subject of purchase; and such a purchase is by reason of My commands invalid.

O Dear One! in the borrowing of barley, wheat, or paddy, the profit of the lender at the end of the year is laid down to be a fourth of the quantity lent, and in the case of the loan of metals one-eighth. In monetary transactions, agriculture, trade, and in all other transactions, men should ever carry out their undertakings. This is approved by the laws. A servant should be skilful, clean, wakeful, careful and alert, and possess his senses under control. He should, as he desires happiness in this and the next world, regard his master as if he were Vishnu Himself, his master's wife; his own mother, and respect his master's kinsmen and friends. He should know his master's friends to be his friends, and his master's enemies to be his enemies and should ever remain in respectful attendance upon his master, awaiting his orders. He should carefully conceal his master's dishonour, the family dissensions, anything said in private or which would disgrace his master. He should not covet the wealth of his master, but remain ever devoted to his good. He should not make use of bad words or laugh or play in his masters presence. He should not, with lustful mind, even look at the maidservants in his master's house, or lie down with them, or play with them in secret. He should not use his master's bed, seat, carriages, clothes, vessels, shoes, jewels, or weapons. If guilty, he should beg the forgiveness of his master. He should not be forward, impertinent, or attempt to place himself on an equal footing with his master.

Except when in the Bhairavi-chakra or Tattva-chakra persons of all castes should marry in their caste according to the Brahma form, and should eat with their own caste people. O Great Queen! in these two circles, however, marriage in the Shaiva form is ordained, and as regards eating and drinking, no caste distinctions exist.

Shri Devi said:

What is the Bhairavi-chakra, and what is the Tattva-chakra? I desire to hear, and it kindly behoves Thee to speak of them.

Shri Sadashiva said:

O Devi! in the ordinances relating to Kula worship I have spoken of the formation of circles by the excellent worshippers at times of special worship. O Dear One! there is no rule relating to the Bhairavi-chakra. This auspicious circle may at any time be formed. I will now speak of the rites relating to this circle, which benefits the worshippers, and in which, if the Devi be worshipped, She speedily grants the prayers of Her votaries.

The Kulacharyya should spread an excellent mat in a beautiful place, and, after purifying it with the Kama and Astra Vijas, should seat himself upon it. Then the wise one should draw a square with a triangle in it with either vermilion or red sandal wood paste, or simply water. Then, taking a painted jar, and smearing it with curd and sun-dried rice, and placing a vermilion mark on it, let him put a branch or leaves and fruit upon it. Filling it with perfumed water whilst uttering the Pranava, the worshipper should place it on the Mandala, and exhibit before it lights and incense-sticks. The jar should then be worshipped with two fragrant flowers. Ishta-devata should be meditated upon as being in the jar. The ritual should be according to the shortened form. Listen, O Adored of the Immortals! whilst I speak to Thee of the peculiar features of this worship. There is no necessity of placing the wine-cups for the Guru and others. The worshipper should then take such of the elements of worship as he wishes, and place them in front of himself. Then, purifying them with the Weapon Mantra, let him gaze upon them with steadfast eyes.

Then, placing scent and flowers in the wine-jar, let him meditate upon the Ananda-Bhairava and Ananda-Bhairavi in it.

Dhyana

He should meditate upon the Blissful Devi as in first bloom of youth, with a body rosy as the first gleam of the rising Sun. The sweet nectar

80

of Her smiles illumines Her face as beautiful as a full-blown lotus. Decked with jewels, clad in beauteous coloured raiment delighting in dance and song, She with the lotus of her hands makes the signs which confer blessings and dispel fears.

After thus meditating on Blissful Devi, let the worshipper thus meditate upon the Blissful Bhairava.

Dhyana

I meditate upon the Deva Who is white as camphor, Whose eyes are large and beautiful like lotuses, the lustre of Whose body is adorned with celestial raiments and jewels, Who holds in His left hand the cup of nectar, and in the right a ball of Shuddhi.

Having thus meditated upon Them both, and thinking of them in a state of union in the wine-jar, the worshipper should then worship Them therein. With Mantra, beginning with the Pranava and ending with Namah, the names of the Devata being placed between, and with perfume and flower, let him then sanctify the wine

The Kula worshipper should sanctify the wine by repeating over it the Pashadi-trika-vija a hundred and eight times. When the Kali Age is in full sway, in the case of the householder whose mind is entirely engrossed with domestic desires, the three sweets should be substituted in the place of the first element of worship (wine). Milk, sugar, and honey are the three sweets. They should be deemed to be the image of wine, and as such offered to the Deity. Those born in the Kali Age are by their nature weak in intellect, and their minds are distracted by lust. By reason of this they do not recognize the Shakti to be the image of the Deity. Therefore, O Parvati! for such as these let there be, in place of the last element of worship (sexual union), meditation upon the lotus-feet of the Devi and the inward recitation of their Ishta-mantra.

Therefore such of the elements of worship as have been obtained should be consecrated by the recitation over each of them of the same Mantra one hundred times. Let the worshipper, with closed eyes, meditate upon them as suffused by Brahman, then offer them to Kali, and, lastly, eat and drink the consecrated elements. O Gentle One! this is the Bhairavi-chakra, which is not revealed in the other Tantras. I have, however spoken before Thee of it. It is the essence of essences, and more excellent than the best. Parvati! In Bhairavi-chakra and Tattva-chakra the excellent worshipper should be wedded to his Shakti, according to the laws prescribed by Shiva. The Vira who without marriage worships by enjoyment of Shakti is, without doubt, guilty of the sin of going with another man's wife. When the Bhairavi-chakra has been formed, the members thereof are like the best of the twice-born; but when the circle is broken, they revert again to their own respective castes. In this circle there is no distinction of caste nor impurity of food. The heroic worshippers in the circle are My image; there is no doubt of that. In the formation of the circle there is no rule as to time or place or question as to fitness. The necessary articles may be used by whomsoever they may have been brought. Food brought from a long distance, whether it be cooked or uncooked, whether brought by a Vira or a Pashu, becomes pure immediately it is brought within the circle.

While the circle is being formed, all dangers flee in confusion, awed by the Brahmanic lustre of its heroes. Upon the mere hearing that a Bhairavi circle has been formed at any place, fierce Pishachas, Guhyakas, Yakshas, and Vetalas depart afar off in fear. Into the circle come all the holy places, the great and holy places, and with reverence Indra and all the Immortals. Shiva! the place where a circle is formed is a great and holy place, more sacred than each and all the other holy places. Even the Thirty desire the excellent offerings made to Thee in this circle. Whatever the food be, whether cooked or uncooked, and whether brought by a Mlechchha, Chandala, Kirata, or Huna, it becomes pure as soon as it is placed in the hand of a Vira. By the seeing of the circle and of the worshippers therein, who are but images of Myself, men infected with the taint of the Kali Age are liberated from the bonds of the life of a Pashu. When, however the Kali Age is in full sway, the circle should not be concealed. The Vira should at all places and at all times practise Kula rites and make Kula worship.

In the circle all distinction of caste, frivolous talk, levity, garrulity, spitting, and breaking wind should be avoided. Such as are cruel, mischievous, Pashu, sinful, atheists, blasphemers of Kula doctrine, and calumniators of the Kula Scriptures, should not be allowed into the circle. Even the Vira who, induced by affection, fear, or attachment, admits a Pashu into the circle falls from his Kula duty, and goes to hell. All who have sought refuge in the Kula Dharmma, whether Brahmamas, Kshatriyas, Vaishyas, Shudras, or Samanyas, should ever be worshipped like Devas. He who, whilst in the circle, makes, from pride, distinctions of caste, descends to a terrible hell, even though he should have gone to the very end of the Vedanta. How within the circle can there be any fear of sin for Kaulas, who are good and pure of heart and who are manifestly the very image of Shiva?. Vipras and others who are followers of Shiva should, so long as they are within the circle, follow the ordinance of Shiva and the observances prescribed by Him.

Without the circle each should follow his own calling according to his caste and stage of life, and should discharge his duty as a man of the world. One Japa made by a devout man, when seated within the circle, bears the fruit attainable by the performance of a hundred Purashcharana and by Shavasana, Mundasana, and Chitasana. Who can describe the glory of the Bhairavi-chakra? Its formation, though but once only, frees of all sins. The man who for six months worships in such a circle will become a King: he who so worships for a year becomes the conqueror of death, and by the daily performance of such worship he attains to Nirvvana.

What is the need, O Kalika! of saying more? Know this for certain: that for the attainment of happiness in this or the next world there is only the Kula-dharmma, and no other. When the Kali Age is dominant and all religion is abandoned, even a Kaula merits hell by concealment of the Kula-dharmma.

I have spoken of the Bhairavi circle, which is the sole means of attaining enjoyment and final liberation. I will now speak to Thee, O Queen of the Kaulas! of the Tattva circle. Do Thou listen.

The Tattva circle is the king of all circles. It is also called the celestial circle. Only worshippers who have attained to a knowledge of Brahman may take part in it. Only those servants of the Brahman may take part in this circle who have attained to knowledge of Brahman, who are devoted to Brahman, pure of heart, tranquil, devoted to the good of all things, who are unaffected by the external world, who see no differences, but to whom all things are the same, who are merciful, faithful to their vows, and who have realized the Brahman.

O Knower of the Supreme Soul! only those who, possessing the knowledge of the Real, look upon this moving and motionless Existence as one with Brahman, such men are privileged to take part in this circle. They who regard everything in the Tattva circle as Brahman, they alone, O Devi, are qualified to take part therein. In the formation of this circle there is no necessity for placing the wine-jar, no lengthy ritual. It can be formed everywhere in a spirit of devotion to Brahman. O Dearest One! the worshipper of the Brahma-Mantra and a devout believer in Brahman should be the Lord of the circle, which he should form of other worshippers who know the Brahman. In a beautiful and clean place, pleasant to the worshippers, pure seats should be spread with beautiful carpets. There, O Shiva! the Lord of the circle should seat himself with the worshippers of Brahman, and have the elements of worship brought and placed in front of him. The Lord of the Circle should inwardly recite the Mantra, beginning with the Tara and ending with the Prana-vija, a hundred times, and then pronounce the following Mantra over the elements:

Mantra

The act of offering is Brahman. The offering itself is Brahman. The Fire is Brahman. He by whom the offering is made is Brahman. By him who is absorbed in the worship of Brahman is unity with Brahman attained.

All the elements should be purified by the inward recitation of this Mantra seven or three times. Then, with the Brahma-Mantra, making an offering of the food and drink to the Supreme Soul, he should partake thereof with the other worshippers, knowers of the Brahman. O Great Queen! there is no distinction of caste in the Brahma circle, nor rule as to place or time or cup. The ignorant who, through want of care, make distinctions of birth or caste go upon the downward path. And therefore should those excellent worshippers, possessed of the knowledge that the Supreme Brahman pervades all things, perform the rites of the Tattva circle with every care for the attainment of religious merit, fulfilment of desire, wealth, and liberation.

Shri Devi said:

Lord! Thou hast spoken in full of the duties of the householder; it now behoves Thee kindly to speak of the duties appropriate to the ascetic life.

Shri Sadashiva said:

Devi! the stage of life of an Avadhuta is in the Kali Age called Sannyasa. Now listen while I tell thee what should be done.

When an adept in spiritual wisdom has acquired the knowledge of Brahman, and has ceased to care for the things of the world, he should seek refuge in the life of an ascetic. If, however, in order to adopt the life of a wandering mendicant, one abandons an old mother or father, infant children and a devoted wife, or helpless dependents, one goes to hell. All, whether Brahmana, Kshatriya, Vaishya, Shudra, or Samanya are equally entitled to take part in the purificatory ceremony of the Kula ascetic.

After the performance of all the duties of a householder, and after satisfying all dependents, one should go forth from his house indifferent, free from desires, with all his senses conquered. He who wishes thus to leave his house should call together his kinsmen and friends, his neighbours and men of his village, and lovingly ask of them their permission. Having obtained it, and made obeisance to his Ishta-devata, he should go round his village, and then without attachment set forth from his house. Liberated from the bonds of household life, and immersed in exceeding joy, he should approach a Kula ascetic of divine knowledge and pray to him as follows:

"0 Supreme Brahman! all this life of mine has been spent in the discharge of household duties. Do Thou O Lord! be gracious to me in this my adoption of the life of an ascetic".

The religious Preceptor should thereupon satisfy himself that the disciple's duties as a householder have all been accomplished, and, on finding him to be meek and full of discernment, initiate him into the second stage. The disciple should then, with a well-controlled mind, make his ablutions and say his daily prayer, and then, with the object of being absolved from the threefold debt due to them, worship the Devas, the Rishis, and the Pitris.

By the Devas are meant Brahma, Vishnu, and Rudra, with their followers; by the Rishis are meant Sanaka and others, as also the

84

Devarshis and the Brahmarshis. Listen, whilst I now enumerate the ancestors which should be worshipped. The father, paternal grandfather, paternal great-grandfather, mother, the maternal grandfather, and others in the ascending line, and the maternal grandmother and others in the ascending line. Upon the dedication of oneself to the life of an ascetic, the Devas and Rishis should be worshipped in the East, the paternal ancestors in the South, the maternal ancestors in the West. Spreading two seats on each of these sides, beginning from the East, and invoking the Devas and others thereto, they should there be worshipped. Having worshipped them in proper form, pindas should be offered to each of them separately according to the rules relating thereto; And then, with folded palms, let the disciple thus supplicate the Devas and Ancestors:

Mantra

O Fathers! O Mothers! O Devas! O Rishis! be you satisfied. Do you absolve me, about to enter upon the path of renunciation from all debts.

Having thus prayed to be free from all debts, bowing again and again, and being thus freed of all debts, he should perform his own funeral rites. The father and paternal grandfather and great-grandfather are one soul. In offering, therefore, the individual soul to the Supreme Soul, he who is wise should perform his own funeral rites. O Devi! sitting with his face to the North, and invoking the spirits of his ancestors upon the seats which he has prepared for them, he should, after doing them homage, offer the funeral cakes. In so offering he should spread kusha grass with its end towards the East, South, West, and towards the North for himself. After completion, according to the directions of the Guru, of the funeral rites, the seeker after emancipation should, in order to purify his heart inwardly, recite the following Mantra a hundred times:

Mantra

Hring, let us worship the Three-eyed One whose fame is fragrant, the Augmenter of increase. May I, as the urvaruka is freed of its stalk, be liberated from death unto immortality.

Then the religious Preceptor should draw a figure on the altar of a shape in accordance with the divinity about to be worshipped and then place the jar on the altar and commence worship. Then the Guru, possessed of divine knowledge, should meditate upon the Supreme Spirit in the manner prescribed by Shambhu, and after worship place fire on the altar. The Guru should then offer unto the fire so sanctified the oblation according to the Sangkalpa, and then make his disciple perform the complete homa. He should first offer oblation with the Vyahritis, and then with the vital airs, prana, apana, samana, udana, vyana.

For the destruction of the false belief that the body, whether gross or subtle, is the Atma, the Tattva-Homa should be performed, uttering the following words:

Mantra

Earth, water, fire, air, ether, (then) scent, taste, vision, touch, sound, (then) speech, hands, feet, anus and organ of generation, (then) ears, skin, eyes, tongue, and smell, (then) manas, buddhi, ahangkara, and chitta, (and lastly) all the functions of the senses and of life.

He should then say:

"May they be purified;" (adding) "May I be like unto the universal Chaitanya united with Hring. May I be like the Light beyond and above Rajo-guna, and may I be free of the taint of ignorance".

Having consigned as oblations into the fire the twenty-four tattvas and the functions of the body, he who is now devoid of all action should consider his body as dead. Considering his body as dead and devoid of all function, and calling to mind the Supreme Brahman, let him take off his sacred thread. He, the possessor of divine knowledge, should take it from his shoulder, uttering the

Mantra

Aing Kling Hangsa.

Holding it in his hand while he recites the three Vyahritis, ending with Svaha, let him throw it steeped in ghee into the fire. Having thus offered the sacred thread as an oblation to the fire, he should, whilst uttering the Kama Vija, cut off his crown-lock and take and place it in the ghee.

Mantra

O Crown Lock! Daughter of Brahman! thou art an ascetic in the form of hair. I am now placing thee in the Purifying One. Depart, O Devi! I make obeisance to thee.

He should then, whilst uttering the Kama, Maya, Kurcha, and Astra Vijas, ending with the word Svaha, make the Homa sacrifice of that lock of hair in the well-sanctified fire. The Pitris, Devas, and Devarshis, as also all acts performed in the stages of life, reside in that lock and have it as their support.

Therefore the man who renounces the crown-lock and sacred thread after the performance of the oblation becomes one with Brahman. The twice-born enter the stage of an ascetic by renunciation of the crown-lock and sacred thread, and the Shudras and Samanyas by the renunciation of the crown-lock only. Then he whose crown-lock and

86

sacred thread have been thus removed should make obeisance to the Guru, laying himself full length upon the ground. The Guru should then raise his disciple and say into his right ear: "O wise one! thou art That." "Think within thyself that I am He and He is I. Free from all attachments and sense of self, do thou go as thou pleasest as moved thereto by thy nature". The Guru, full of the knowledge of the Divine essence, should then, after removal of the jar and the fire, bow to the disciple, recognizing in him his own very self, and say: "O Thou whose form is this Universe! I bow to Thee and to myself. Thou art 'That' and 'That' is Thou. Again I bow to thee.".

The worshippers of the Brahma-Mantra, possessed of divine knowledge, who have conquered themselves, attain the stage of an ascetic by cutting off the crown-lock with their own Mantra. What need is there for those purified by divine knowledge of sacrificial or funeral rites or ritual worship? For they, acting as they please, are never guilty of any fault. The disciple, image of the absence of all contraries, desireless, and of tranquil mind, may, as he pleases, roam the earth, the visible image of Brahman. He will think of everything, from Brahma to a blade of grass, as the image of the existent one, and, oblivious of his own name and form, he will meditate upon the Supreme Soul in himself. Homeless, merciful, fearless, devoid of attachment claiming nothing as his own, devoid of egoism, the ascetic will move about the earth. He is free of all prohibitions. He shall not strive to attain what he has not, nor to protect what he has. He knows himself. He is equally unaffected by either joy or sorrow. He is calm, the conqueror of himself, and free from all desires.

His soul is untroubled even in sorrow, desireless even in prosperity. He is ever joyful, pure, calm, indifferent and unperturbed. He will hurt no living thing, but will be ever devoted to the good of all being. He is free from anger and fear, with his senses under control and without desire. He strives not for the preservation of his body. He is not obsessed by any longing. He will be free from grief and resentment, equal to friend and foe, patient in the endurance of cold and heat, and to him both honour and disgrace are one and the same. He is the same in good or evil fortune, pleased with whatsoever, without effort, he may obtain. He is beyond the three attributes, of unconditioned mind free of covetousness, and (wealth) he will hoard not. He will be happy in the knowledge that, as the unreal universe exists dependent upon the Truth, so does the body depend upon the soul. He attains liberation by the realization that the soul is completely detached from the organs of sense, and is the witness of that which is done.

The ascetic should not accept any metal, and should avoid calumny, untruth, jealousy, all play with woman, and all discharge of seed. He should regard with an equal eye worms, men, and Devas. The religious mendicant should know that in everything he does, in that is Brahman. He should eat without making any distinction of place, time, person, or vessel, and whether from the hand of a Vipra or Chandala, or from any other person whatsoever. The ascetic, thouugh passing his time as he pleases, should study the Scriptures relating to the Soul and in meditation upon the nature of That. The corpse of an ascetic should on no account be cremated. It should be worshipped with scents and flowers, and then either buried or sunk into water. O Devi! the inclination of those men who have not attained union with the Supreme Soul and who ever seek after enjoyment, is by nature turned towards the path of action.

They remain attached to the practice of meditation, ritual worship, and recitation. Let them who are strong in their faith therein know that to be the best for them. It is on account of them that I have spoken of various rites for the purification of the heart, and have with the same object devised many names and forms. O Devi! without knowledge of the Brahman and the abandonment of all ritual worship, man cannot attain emancipation even though he performed countless such acts of worship. The householder should consider the Kula ascetic, possessed of divine knowledge, to be the visible Narayana in the form of man, and should worship Him as such. By the mere sight of one who has subdued his passions a man is freed of all his sins, and earns that merit which he obtains by journeying to places of pilgrimage, the giving of alms, and the performance of all vows, penances, and sacrifices

End of the Eighth Joyful Message, entitled "The Dharmma and Customs of the Castes and Ashramas."

Chapter 9

The Ten Kinds of Purificatory Rites (Sangskara)

THE Adorable Sadashiva said:

O Virtuous One! I have spoken to Thee of the custom and religious duties appropriate to the different castes and stages of life. Do thou now listen whilst I tell Thee of the purificatory rites of the different castes. Without such rites, O Devi! the body is not purified, and he who is not purified may not perform the ceremonies relating to the Devas and the Pitris. Therefore it is that men of every caste, commencing with the Vipras, who desire their welfare in this life and hereafter, should, in all things and with care, perform the purificatory rites which have been ordained for their respective castes.

The ten purificatory ceremonies are those relating to conception, pregnancy, and birth of the child; the giving of its name, its first view of the sun, its first eating of rice, tonsure, investiture, and marriage.

The Shudras and mixed castes have no sacred thread, and but nine purificatory ceremonies; for the twice-born classes there are ten. O Beautiful Lady! all observances, whether they be obligatory, occasional, or voluntary, should be performed according to the injunctions of Shambhu. O Dearest One! I have already, in My form of Brahma, spoken of the rules appropriate to the purificatory and other observances, and of the Mantras appropriate to the various purificatory and other observances, according to the differences in caste.

In the Satya, Treta, and Dvapara Ages, the Mantras, O Kalika! were in their application preceded by the Pranava; but in the Kali Age, O Supreme Devi! the decree of Shangkara is that man do perform all rites with the aid of the same Mantras, but preceded by the Maya Vija. All Mantras in the Nigamas, Agamas, Tantras, Sanghitas and Vedas, have been spoken by Me. Their employment, however, varies according to the Ages. For the benefit of men of the Kali Age, men bereft of energy and dependent for existence on the food they eat, the Kula doctrine, O Auspicious One! is given.

I will now speak to Thee in brief of the purificatory and other rites, suitable for the weak men of the Kali Age, whose minds are incapable of continued effort. Kushandika precedes all auspicious ceremonies. I shall, therefore, O Adored of the Devas! speak firstly of it. Do Thou listen. In a clean and pleasant spot, free from husks and charcoal, let the wise one make a square, the sides of which are of one cubit's length. Then draw in it three lines from the West to East (of the square). Let him then sprinkle water over them, uttering the Kurcha Vija the while. Then Fire should be brought to the accompaniment of the Vahni Vija. The Fire, when so brought, should be placed by the side of the square, the worshipper breathing the Vagbhava Vija. Then, taking up a piece of burning wood with the right hand from the Fire, he should put it aside as the share of the Rakshasas, saying:

Mantra

Hring, Salutation to the raw-meat eaters: Svaha.

The worshipper, lifting up the consecrated Fire with both hands, should place it in front of him on the three lines (above mentioned), inwardly reciting the while the Maya Vija before the Vyahritis. Grass and wood should then be thrown upon the Fire to make it blaze, and two pieces of wood should be smeared with ghee and offered as an oblation to it. Thereafter Fire should be named according to the object of worship, and then meditated upon as follows:

Dhyana

Ruddily effulgent like the young Sun, with seven tongues and two crowned heads of matted hair, seated on a goat, whose weapon is Shakti.

Having so meditated upon the Carrier of oblations, He should be thus invoked with joined palms.

Mantra

Having thus invoked Him, the worshipper should say, "O Fire! this is Thy seat," and then worship him, the Seven-tongued, with appropriate offerings. The seven licking Tongues of Fire are: Kali, Karali, Mano-java, Sulohita, Su-dhumra-varna, Sphulingini, and Vishva-nirupini. Then, O Great Devi! the sides of the Fire should be thrice sprinkled with water from the hand, beginning from the East and ending at the North. Then the sides of the Fire, from the South to the North, should be thrice sprinkled with water, and following that the articles of sacrifice should be thrice sprinkled. Then spread kusha grass on the sides of the square, beginning with the East and ending with the North. The ends of the blades of grass on the North should be turned towards the North, and the rest of the grass should be placed with its ends towards the East. The worshipper should then proceed to the seat placed for Brahma, keeping the Fire on his right, and, picking up with his left thumb and little finger a blade of kusha grass from the seat of Brahma, should throw it along with the remaining blades of kusha grass on the South side of the fire, uttering the

Mantra

"Hring, Destroy the abode of the enemy".

(The performer of the sacrifice should then say to Brahma:) " O Brahman, Lord of Sacrifices, be thou seated here. This seat is made for thee." The Brahma, saying "I sit," should then sit down, with his face turned towards the North. After worshipping Brahma with scent, flowers, and the other articles of worship, let him be supplicated thus:

Mantra

O Lord of Sacrifices! protect the sacrifice.O Brihaspati! protect this sacrifice. Protect me also, the performer of this sacrifice.O Witness of all acts! I bow to Thee.

Brahma should then say, "I protect," and if there is no person representing Brahma, then the performer of the sacrifice should, for the success of the sacrifice, make an image with darbha grass of the Vipra, and himself say this. The worshipper should then invoke Brahma, saying, "0 Brahman, come here, come here!" and, after doing honour to him by offering water for washing his feet and the like, let him supplicate him, saying, "So long as this sacrifice be not concluded, do Thou deign to remain here," and then make obeisance to him. He should then sprinkle the space between the North-East corner of the fire and the seat of Brahma three times with water taken in his hand, and should thereafter sprinkle the fire also three times, and then, returning the way he went, take his own seat. Let him then spread on the North side of the square some darbha grass, with the ends of the blades towards the North. He should then place thereon the articles necessary for the sacrifice, such as the vessel (filled with water) for sprinkling, and the vessel containing ghee, sacrificial fuel, and kusha grass. He should also place the sacrificial ladle and spoon on the darbha grass, and purify them by sprinkling water over them, and then, regarding them with a celestial gaze, uttering the

Mantra

Hrang Hring Hrung.

Then, with his right knee touching the ground, let him put ghee into the spoon with the ladle, and, with desire for his own well-being, Jet him offer three oblations, saying the

Mantra

Hring to Vishnu. Svaha (4o).

Taking again ghee in the same way, and meditating upon Prajapati, oblations should be offered with ghee streaked across the fire from the corner of Agni to that of Vayu. Taking ghee again and meditating on Indra, let him offer oblations from the corner of Nairrita to that of Ishana. O Devi! oblations should thereafter be offered to the North, the South, and to the middle of the fire, to Agni, Soma, and to Agni and Soma together. Upon that three oblations should be offered, uttering the

Mantras

Hring salutation to Agni,

Hring salutation to Soma,

Hring salutation to both Agni and Soma,

respectively. Having performed these (preliminary) rites, the wise one should proceed to that prescribed for the Homa sacrifice, which is to be performed. The offering of oblations (as above described), commencing with the three offerings made to Vishnu and ending with the offering to Agni and Soma, is called Dhara Homa.

When making any offering, both the Deva, to which the same is being made, and the thing offered should be mentioned, and upon the conclusion of the principal rite he should perform the Svishti-krit Homa. O Beautiful One! in the Kali Age there is no Prayashchitta Homa. The object thereof is attained by Svishti-krit and Vyahriti Homas. O Devi! (for Svishti-krit Homa.) ghee should be taken in manner above mentioned, and, whilst mentally reciting the name of Brahma, oblation should be offered with the following:

Mantra

Hring, O Deva of the Devas! do Thou make faultless any shortcomings that there may be in this rite, and anything done needlessly, whether by negligence or mistake. Svaha.

Then oblation should be offered to Fire, thus:

Mantra

Hring, O Fire! Thou art the Purificator of all things. Thou makest all sacrifices propitious, and art the Lord of all. Thou art the Witness of all sacrificial rites, and the Insurer of their success. Do Thou fulfil all my desires.

The sacrificing priest, having thus concluded the Svishti-krit Homa, should thus (pray to the Supreme Brahman):

Mantra

O Supreme Brahman! O Omnipresent One! for the removal of the effects of whatsoever has been improperly done in this sacrifice, and for the success of the sacrifice, I am making this Vyahriti Homa.

Saying this, he should offer three oblations with the three

Mantras

Hring Bhuh Svaha,

Hring Bhuvah Svaha,

Hring Svah Svaha.

Thereafter offering one more oblation with the

Mantra

Hring Bhuh, Bhuvah, Svah Svaha,

the wise priest should, jointly with the giver of the sacrifice, offer the complete oblation. If the latter has performed the sacrifice without a priest, he should offer the oblation himself. This is the rule in Abhisheka and other observances. The Mantra for the complete oblation is –

Mantra

Hring, O Lord of Sacrifice! may this Sacrifice of mine be complete. May all the Devatas of sacrifices be pleased and grant that which is desired. Svaha.

The learned one should, after offering the complete oblation, perform Shanti-karma. Taking water from the sprinkling vessel, he should with kusha grass sprinkle it over the heads of the persons present, reciting the

Mantra

May the water be friendly to me, may water be like a medicament to me, may water preserve me always; water is Narayana Himself. Do thou, O water! grant me happiness and my earthly desires, and so forth.

Having said this, and sprinkled water over the heads of those present, throw a few drops on the ground, saying:

Mantra

To those who are ever hostile to me, and to those to whom we are ever hostile, may water be their enemy and engulf them.

Sprinkling a few drops of water in the North-East corner to the accompaniment of the above-mentioned Mantra, the kusha grass should be put away, and supplication should be made to the Carrier of oblations as follows:

Mantra

O Carrier of Oblations! do Thou grant unto me understanding, knowledge, strength, intelligence, wisdom, faith, fame, fortune, health, energy, and long life.

Having thus prayed to Fire, he should, O Shiva! be bidden to depart with the following:

Mantra

Sacrifice! do thou depart to the Lord of Sacrifice.

Fire! do thou depart to the Sacrifice itself.

Lord of Sacrifice! do Thou depart to Thine own place and fulfil my desires.

Then saying, "Fire, forgive me," the Fire should be moved to the South by pouring oblations of curd on the North of Fire. Then the worshipper should give a present to Brahma, and, after bowing to him respectfully, bid him go, and, with the ashes adhering to the ladle, the officiating priest should then make a mark on his own forehead and on that of the giver of the sacrifice, uttering the

Mantra

Hring, Kling, do thou bring peace; mayest thou cause prosperity. By the grace of Indra, of Agni, of the Maruts, Brahma, the Vasus, the Rudras, and Praja-pati, may there be peace, may there be prosperity.

Whilst saying this Mantra, he should place a flower on his own head. Thereafter the giver of the sacrifice should, as his means allow, offer presents for the success of the sacrifice and for the Kushandika rite.

I have spoken to Thee, O Devi! of Kushandika, which is the groundwork of all auspicious ceremonies, and which all Kula worshippers should with care perform at the commencement thereof.

O Auspicious One! I will now speak to Thee of Charu-karma, in order to insure the ritual success in those families in which the cooking of charu is a traditional practice in the performance of all rites. The pot for cooking charu should be made of either copper or mud. In the first place, the articles should be consecrated according to the rules prescribed in Kushandika, and then the pot of charu should be placed in front of the worshipper. After careful examination to see that it is without holes and unbroken, a blade of kusha grass of the length of a pradesha should be put in the pot. The rice should be placed near the square and then, O Adored of the Devas! the names of such of the Devas as are to be worshipped in each particular ceremony should be uttered in the dative case, followed by the words "to please Thee," and then "I take," "I place it in the pot," and "I put water into it," and put four handfuls of rice in the name of each Deva. He should then take the rice, put it in the pot, and pour water over it. O Virtuous One! milk and sugar should be added thereto, as is done in cooking. The whole should then be well and carefully cooked over the consecrated fire. And when he is satisfied that it is well cooked and soft, the sacrificial ladle, filled with ghee, should be let into it. Thereafter placing the pot on kusha grass on the northern side of the Fire, and adding ghee to the charu three times, the pot should be covered with blades of kusha grass. Then, putting a little ghee into the sacrificial spoon, a little charu should be taken from the pot. With it Janu Homa is done. Then, after doing Dhara Homa, oblations should be made with the Mantras of the Devas, who are directed to be worshipped in the principal rite. Completing the principal Homa after performance of Svishti-krit Homa, expiatory Homa should be performed, and the rite thus completed. In the sacramental and consecratory ritual this is the method to be observed. In all auspicious ceremonies it should be followed for the complete success thereof.

Now, O Mahamaya! I will speak of Garbhadhana and other rites. I will speak of them in their order, beginning with Ritusangskara. Do Thou listen.

After performing his daily duties and purifying himself, (the priest) should worship the five deities—Brahma, Durga, Ganesha, the Grahas, and the Dikpalas. They should be worshipped in the jars on the East side of the square, and then the sixteen Matrikas—namely, Gauri and others—should be worshipped in their order. The sixteen Matrikas are Gauri, Padma, Shachi, Medha, Savitri, Vijaya, Jaya, Deva-sena, Svadha, Svaha, Shanti, Pushti, Dhriti, Kshama, the worshipper's own tutelary Devata, and the family Devata.

Mantra

May the Mothers that cause the joy of the Devas come and bring all success to weddings, vratas, and yajnas. May they come upon their respective carriers, and in all the fulness of their power, in their benign aspect, and add to the glory of this festival.

Having thus invoked the Mothers and worshipped them to the best of his powers, the priest should make five or seven marks with vermilion and sandal paste on the wall, at the height of his navel, and within the space of a pradesha.

The wise one should then, whilst breathing the three Vijas–Kling, Hring, and Shring–pour an unbroken stream of ghee from each of the said marks, and there worship the Deva Vasu. The wise man, having thus made the Vasu-dhara according to the directions which I have given, and having made the square and placed the Fire thereupon, and consecrated the articles requisite for Homa, should then cook the excellent charu. Charu which is cooked in this (Ritu-sangskara) is called Prajapatya, and the name of this Fire is Vayu. After concluding Dhara Homa, the rite of Ritu-sangs-kara should be begun. Three oblations of charu should be offered with the

Mantra

Hring. salutation to Prajapati. Svaha.

The one oblation should be offered with the following:

Mantra

May Vishnu grant the power to conceive. May Tvashta give the form. May Prajapati sprinkle it, and may Dhata give the power to bear.

This oblation should be made with either ghee or charu, or with ghee and charu, and should be offered meditating upon the Sun, Vishnu, and Prajapati.

Mantra

May Sinibali give support to thy womb, may Sarasvati give support to thy womb, may the two Ashvins, who wear garlands of lotuses, give support to thy womb.

Meditating upon the Devis Sinibali and Sarasvati and the two Ashvins, excellent oblations should be offered with the above Mantra, followed by Svaha. Then oblation should be offered to the sanctified Fire, meditating upon Surya and Vishnu with the

Mantra

Kling, String, Hring, Shring, Hung, grant conception to her, who desires a son: Svaha.

Then, in the name of Vishnu, oblations should be offered with the following:

96

Mantra

As this extended Earth ever carries a full womb, do thou likewise carry for ten months until delivery. Svaha.

Meditating upon the Supreme Vishnu, let a little more ghee be thrown into the Fire with the following:

Mantra

Vishnu! do Thou in Thy excellent form put into this woman an excellent son: Svaha.

And, uttering the following

Mantra

Kling, Hring, Kling, Hring, String, Hring, Kling, Hring,

let the husband touch his wife's head. Then the husband, surrounded by a few married women having sons, should place both hands on the head of his wife, and, after meditating on Vishnu, Durga, Vidhi and Surya, place three fruits on the cloth of her lap. Thereupon he should bring the ceremony to a close by making Svishti-krit oblations and expiatory rites. Or the wife and husband may be purified by worshipping Gauri and Shangkara in the evening, and by giving oblations to Sun.

I have now spoken of Ritu-sangskara. Now listen to that relating to Garbhadhana. On the same night, or on some night having a date of an even number, after the ceremony, the husband should enter the room with his wife, and, meditating on Prajapati, should touch his wife and say:

Mantra

Hring, O Bed! be thou propitious for the begetting of a good offspring of us two.

He should then with the wife get on the bed, and there sit with his face towards the East or the North. Then, looking at his wife, let him embrace her with his left arm, and, placing his right hand over her head, let him make japa of the Mantra on the different parts of her body (as follows): Let him make japa over the head of the Kama Vija a hundred times; over her chin of the Vagbhava Vija a hundred times; over the throat of the Rama Vija twenty times; and the same Vija a hundred times over each of her two breasts. He should then recite the Maya Vija ten times over her heart, and twenty-five times over her navel. Next let him place his hand on her member, and recite jointly the

97

Kama and Vagbhava Vijas a hundred and eight times, and let him similarly recite the same Vijas over his own member a hundred and eight times; and then, saying the Vija "Hring," let him part the lips of her member, and let him go into her with the object of begetting a child. The husband should, at the time of the spending of his seed, meditate on Brahma, and, discharging it below the navel into the Raktikanadi in the Chitkunda, he should at the same time recite the following (114, 115):

Mantra

As the Earth is pregnant of Fire, as the Heaven is pregnant of Indra, as the Points of the compass are pregnant of the Air they contain, so do thou also become pregnant (by this my seed).

If the wife then, or at a subsequent period, conceive, the householder, O Maheshvari! should perform in the third month after conception the Pungsavana rite. After the performance of his daily duties, the husband should worship the five Devas and the heavenly Mothers, Gauri and others, and should make the Vasu-dhara.

The wise one should then perform Briddhi Shraddha, and, as aforementioned, the ceremonies up to Dhara-Homa, and then proceed to the Pungsavana rites. The charu prepared for Pungsavana is called "Prajapatya," and the fire is called Chandra. One grain of barley and two Masha beans should be put into curd made from cow's milk, and this should be given to the wife to drink, and, whilst she is drinking it, she should be asked three times: "What is that thou art drinking,O gentle one?". The wife should make answer: "Hring, I am drinking that which will cause me to bear a son." In this manner the wife should drink three mouthfuls of the curd. The wife should then be led by women whose husbands and children are living to the place of sacrifice, and the husband should there seat her on his left and proceed to perform Charu-Homa.

Taking a little charu as aforementioned, and uttering the Maya Vija and the Kurcha Vija, he should offer it as oblation, with the following:

Mantra

Do thou destroy, do thou destroy all these Bhutas, Pretas, Pishachas, and Vetalas, who are inimical to conception and destroyers of the child in the womb, and of the young. Do thou protect (the child in) the womb, do thou protect (the child in) the womb.

Whilst reciting the above Mantra, meditate upon Fire, as Raksko-ghna, and on Rudra and Prajapati, and then offer twelve oblations.

He should then offer five oblations with the

Mantra

Hring, Salutation to Chandra. Svaha.

And then, touching his wife's heart, breathe inwardly the Vijas Hring and Shring one hundred times. He should then perform Svishti-krit Homa and Prayash-chitta, and complete the ceremony. Panchamrita should be given in the fifth month of pregnancy 128). Sugar, honey, milk, ghee, and curd in equal quantities make Panchamrita. It is needful for the purification of the body. Breathing the Vijas Aing, Kling, Shring, Hring, Hung, and Lang, five times over each of the five ingredients, the husband, after mixing them together, should cause his wife to eat it. Then, in the sixth or eighth month, the Simantonnayana rite should be performed. It may, however, be performed any time before the child is born. The wise one should, after performing the rites as aforementioned, do Dhara-Homa, and sit with his wife on a seat, and offer three oblations to Vishnu, Surya, and Brahma, saying:

Mantra

To Vishnu Svaha, to the Effulgent One Svaha, to Brahma Svaha.

Then, meditating on Chandra, let him offer seven oblations to Soma into Fire under his name of Shiva. Then, O Shiva! he should meditate upon the Ashwins, Vasava, Vishnu, Shiva, Durga, Prajapati and offer five oblations to each of them. The husband should after that take a gold comb, and comb back the hair on each side of the head and tie it up with the chignon. He should, whilst so combing the hair, meditate upon Shiva, Vishnu. and Brahma, and pronounce the Maya Vija and the

Mantra

O Wife! thou auspicious and fortunate one, thou of auspicious vows! do thou in the tenth month, by the grace of Vishva-karma, be safely delivered of a good child. May thou live long and happy. This comb, may it give thee strength and prosperity!

Saying this Mantra, the ceremony should be completed with Svishti-krit Homa and other rites. Immediately after the birth of the son the wise one should look upon his face and present him with a piece of gold, and then in another room perform Dhara Homa in the manner already described. He should then offer five oblations to Agni, Indra, Prajapati, the Vishva-devas, and Brahma.

The father should thereafter mix equal quantities of honey and ghee in a bell-metal cup, and, breathing the Vagbhava Vija over it a hundred times, make the child swallow it. It should be put into the child's mouth with the fourth finger of the right hand, with the following:

Mantra

Child, may thy life, vitality, strength, and intelligence ever increase.

After performing this rite for the longevity of the child, the father should give him a secret name, by which at the time of the investiture with the sacred thread he should be called. The father should then finish the Jata-karma by the performance of the usual expiatory and other rites, and then the midwife should with firmness cut the umbilical cord. The period of uncleanliness commences only after the cord is cut; therefore all rites relating to the Devas and the Pitris should be performed before the cord is cut. If a daughter is born, all the acts as above indicated are to be performed, but the Mantras are not to be said. In the sixth or eighth month the boy should be given the name by which he is usually known. At the time of naming of the child the mother should, after bathing him and dressing him in two pieces of fine cloth, come to and place him by the side of her husband, with his face towards the East. The father should thereupon sprinkle the head of the child with water taken up upon blades of kusha grass and gold, saying at the time the following:

Mantra

May Jahnavi, Yamuna, Reva, the holy Sarasvati, Narmada, Varada, Kunti, the Oceans and Tanks, Lakes–all these bathe thee for the attainment of Dharmma, Kama, and Artha.

O Waters! thou art the Pranava, and thou givest all happiness. Do thou therefore provide for us food in (this) world, and do thou also enable us to see the Supreme and Beautiful (Para-brahman). Water! thou art not different from the Pranava. Grant that we may enjoy in this world thy most beneficent essence. Your wishes arise of themselves spontaneously like those of mothers. Water! thou art the very form of Pranava. We go to enjoy to our fill that essence of thine by which thou satisfieth (this Universe). May thou bring us enjoyment therein.

The wise one should sprinkle water over the child, with the three preceding Mantras, and then, as aforesaid, consecrate the fire and perform the rites leading up to Dhara Homa in the manner already described, and then should offer five oblations. He should make the oblation to Agni, then to Vasava, then to Prajapati, then to the Vishva-Devas, and then to Yahni under his name of Parthiva.

Then, taking the son in his lap, the prudent father should speak into his right ear an auspicious name–one that is short, and that can easily be pronounced. After whispering the name three times into the son's ear, he should inform the Brahmanas who are present of it, and then conclude the ceremony with Svishtikrit Homa and the other concluding rites.

For a daughter there is no Nishkramana, nor is Vriddhi Shraddha necessary. The wise man performs the naming, the giving of the first rice, and tonsure of a daughter without any Mantra.

In the fourth or sixth month after birth the Nishkramana Sangskara ceremony of the son should be performed.

After performing his daily duties, the father should, after bathing, worship Ganesha, and then bathe and adorn his son with clothes and jewels, and, placing him in front of himself, pronounce the following:

Mantra

Brahma, Vishnu, Shiva, Durga, Ganesha, Bhaskara, Indra, Vayu, Kuvera, Varuna, Agni, and Brihaspati, may They always be propitious to this child, and may They always protect him throughout his going forth from the house.

Having said this, he should take the child in his arms, and, preceded by vocal and instrumental music, and surrounded by his rejoicing kinsmen, take the son out of the house. Going a little distance, he should show the Sun to the child, with the following:

Mantra

Ong, yonder is the Eye (of Heaven) who excels even Shukra in his effulgence, who is beneficent even to the Devas. May we see him a hundred years. May we live a hundred years.

Having shown the Sun to his child, the father should return to his own house, and, after making offering to the Sun, feast his kinsmen. O Shiva! in the sixth or eighth month either the father's brother or the father himself should give the first rice to the child. After worshipping the Devas and purifying fire as aforementioned, and duly performing the ceremonies leading to Dhara Homa, the father should make five oblations to Fire, under his name of Shuchi, to each of the following Devas: He should make the oblations first to Agni, next to Vasava, after him to Prajapati, then to the Vishva-devas, and then the fifth ahuti to Brahma. He should then meditate upon the Devi Annada, and, after giving Her five oblations in Fire, place the son, adorned with clothes and jewels, in his lap, and give him payasa, either in the same or in another room. The payasa should be put into the child's mouth five times, uttering the Mantras for making oblations to the five vital airs; and after that a little rice and curry should be put into the child's mouth. The ceremony should be brought to a close by the blowing of conches and horns and other music, and by performing the concluding expiatory rite.

I have done speaking of the rice-eating ceremony. I shall now speak of the tonsure ceremony. Do Thou listen.

101

In the third or fifth year, according to the custom in the family, the tonsure of the boy should be performed for the success of the sacramental rites of the boy. The wise father should, after concluding the preliminary rites leading up to Dhara Homa, place on the north side of the Fire, called Satya, a mud platter filled with cow-dung, tila-seeds, and wheat, also a little lukewarm water and a keen-edged razor.

The father should place the son on his mother's lap, the mother sitting on her husband's left, and, after breathing the Varuna Vija ten times over the water, rub the hair of the boy's head with lukewarm water. He should then tie the hair with two blades of kusha grass into a knot, uttering meanwhile the Maya Vija. Then, saying the Maya and Lakshmi Vijas three times, he should cut off the knot with the steel razor and place it in the hands of the child's mother. The boy's mother should then take it with both hands and place it in the platter containing the cow-dung, and the father should then say to the barber: "Barber, do thou at thine ease proceed with the shaving of the boy's hair, Svaha." Then, looking at the barber, he should make three oblations to Prajapati, into Vahni, under his name of Satya. After the boy has been shaved by the barber he should be bathed and adorned with clothes and jewels, and placed near the fire on the left of his mother, and the father should, after performance of Svishti-krit Homa and the expiatory rites, offer the complete oblation. Then, uttering the following:

Mantra

Hring, O Child! may the omnipresent Creator of the Universe grant thee well-being,

he should pierce the ears of the boy with gold or silver needles. He should then sprinkle the child with water, uttering the

Mantra

O Water! thou art, etc. (aforementioned);

and, after performing Shanti Karma and other rites, and making presents, bring the ceremony to a close. The sacramental rites from Garbhadhana to Chudakarana are common to all castes. But for Shudras and Samanyas they must be performed without Mantras.

In the case of the birth of a daughter all castes are to perform the rites without Mantras. In the case of a daughter there is no Nishkramana.

I will now speak of the Sacred Thread Ceremony of the twice-born classes, by which the twice-born become qualified for performing rites relating to the Devas and Pitris.

In the eighth year from conception, or the eighth year after birth, the boy should be invested with the sacred thread. After the sixteenth year the son should not be invested, and one so invested is disqualified for all rites.

The learned man should, after finishing his daily duties, worship the five Devas, as also the Matrikas, Gauri, and others, and make the Vasudhara. He should thereafter perform Briddhi Shraddha for the satisfaction of the Devas and Pitris, and perform the rites, ending with Dhara Homa, as directed in the performance of Kushandika.

The boy should be given a little to eat; then his head, with the exception of the crown lock, should be shaved, and after that he should be well bathed and decked with jewels and silken clothes.

The boy should then be taken to the Chhaya-mandapa, near Fire, under his name of Samudbhava, and there made to sit on a clean seat to the left (of his father or Guru). The Guru should say: "My son, dost thou adopt Brahma-charyya?" The disciple should say respectfully: "I do adopt it". The Preceptor should then with a cheerful mind give two pieces of Kashaya cloth for the long life and strength of mind of the gentle boy. Then when the boy has put on the Kashaya cloth, he should, without speaking, give him a knotted girdle made of three strings of munja or kusha grass. On that the boy should say, "Hring, may this auspicious girdle prove propitious"; and, saying this, and putting it round his waist, let him sit in silence before the Guru.

Mantra

This sacrificial thread is very sacred; Brihaspati of old wore it. Do thou wear this excellent white sacrificial thread which contributes to prolong life. May it be for thee strength and courage.

With this Mantra the boy should be given a sacrificial thread made of the skin of the black buck, as also a staff made of bamboo, or a branch of Khadira, Palasha, or Kshira trees. When the boy has put the sacred thread round his neck and holds the staff in his hand, the Guru should three times recite the

Mantra

"O Water! thou art," etc. (aforementioned),

preceded and followed by Hring, and should sprinkle the boy with water taken with kusha grass, and fill the joined palms of the latter with water. After the boy has offered the water to Suryya, the Guru should show the boy the Sun, and recite the

Mantra.

"Yonder is the Sun," etc. (aforementioned).

After the boy has viewed the Sun, the Guru should address him as follows: "My Son! place thy mind on my observances. I bestow upon thee my disposition. Do thou follow the observances with an undivided mind. May my word contribute to thy well-being". After saying this, the Guru, touching the boy's heart, should ask, "My Son! what is thy name?" and the boy should make reply: " . . . Sharmma, I bow to thee". And to the question of the Guru, "Whose Brahma-chari art thou?" the disciple will reverently answer: "I am thy Brahma-chari". The Guru should thereupon say: "Thou art the Brahma-chari of Indra, and Fire is thy Guru." Saying this, the good Guru should consign him to the protection of the Devas. "My Son! I give thee to Prajapati, to Savitri, to Varuna, to Prithivi, to the Vishva-devas, and to all the Devas. May they all ever protect thee".

The boy should thereafter go round the sacrificial fire and the preceptor, keeping both upon his right, and then resume his own seat. The Guru, O Beloved! should then, with his disciple touching him, offer five oblations to Five Devas—namely, Prajapati, Shukra, Vishnu, Brahma, and Shiva. When the oblations are offered into Fire, under his name of Samud-bhava, the names of each of the Devas should be pronounced in the dative, preceded by Hring and followed by Svaha. Where there is no Mantra mentioned, this method is to be followed in all cases. After this, oblation should be offered to Durga, Mahalakshmi, Sundari, Bhuvaneshvari, Indra, and the other nine regents of the quarters, and Bhaskara and the eight planets. The name of each of these should be mentioned whilst the offering of oblations is made. The wise Guru should then cover the boy with cloth, and ask him, who is desirous of attaining Brahma-charyya: "What is the ashrama thou desirest, my son! and what is thy heart's desire?". The disciple should thereupon hold the feet of the Preceptor, and, with a reverent mind, say: "First instruct me in Divine Knowledge, and then in that of the householder".

O Shiva! when the disciple in this manner has thus beseeched his Guru, the latter should three times whisper into his disciple's right ear the Pranava, which contains all the Mantras in itself, and should also utter the three Vyahritis, as also the Savitri. Sadashiva is its Rishi, the verse is Trishtup, the presiding Deva is Savitri, and its object is the attainment of final liberation. The Gayatri Mantra is:

Mantra

Ong, let us contemplate the wonderful Spirit of the Divine Creator. May He direct our understanding, Ong.

This Deva is the Spirit of the three worlds, containing in Himself the three qualities. By the three Vyahritis, therefore, the all-pervading

Brahman is expressed. He Who is expressed by the Pranava and the Vyahritis is also known by the Savitri. Let us meditate upon the sublime, all-pervading eternal Truth, the great immanent and lustrous energy, adored by the self-controlled; Savita, effulgent and omnipresent One, Whose manifested form the world is, the Creator. May Bharga, Who witnesseth all, and is the Lord of all, direct and engage our mind, intelligence, and senses towards those acts, which lead to the attainment of Dharmma, Artha, Kama, and Moksha.

O Devi! the excellent Guru, having thus instructed the disciple, and explained to him the Divine Wisdom, should direct him in the duties of a householder. "My Son! do thou now discard the garments of a Brahma-chari, and honour the Devas and Pitris according to the way revealed by Shambhu". Thy body is sanctified by the instructions thou hast received in Divine Wisdom. Do thou, now that thou hast reached the stage of a householder, engage thyself in thy duties appropriate to that mode of life. Put on two sacred threads, two good pieces of cloth, jewels, shoes, umbrella, fragrant garland, and paste. The disciple should then take off his Kashaya cloth and his sacred thread of black-buck skin and his girdle, and give them and his staff, begging-bowl, and also what has been received by him in the shape of customary alms, to his Guru.

He should then put on two sacred threads and two fine cloths, and wear a garland of fragrant flowers, and perfume himself, and thereafter sit in silence near the Guru, who should address him as follows:

"Conquer the senses, be truthful and devoted to the acquisition of Divine Knowledge and the study of the Vedas, and discharge the duties of a householder according to the rules prescribed in the Dharmma Shastras".

Having thus instructed the disciple, the Guru should make him offer three oblations into Fire in the name of Samudbhava with the

Mantra

Hring, Earth, Firmament, and Heaven, Ong.

He should then himself perform Svishti-krit Homa, and then, O Gentle One! he should bring the investiture ceremony to a close by offering the complete oblation.

Beloved! all ceremonies, from the Jivaseka to Upana-yana ceremonies, are performed by the father alone. The ceremony relating to marriage may be performed either by the father or by the bridegroom himself. The pious man should on the day of marriage perform his ablutions and finish his daily duties, and should then worship the five Devas and the Divine Mothers, Gauri and others, and making the Vasu-dhara do Briddhi Shraddha. At night the betrothed bridegroom, preceded by vocal and musical instrumental music, should be brought to the chhaya-mandapa and seated on an excellent seat. The bridegroom should sit facing the East, and the giver of the bride should face the west, and the latter, after rinsing his mouth, should, with the assisting Brahmanas, say the words "Svasti" and "Riddhi".

The giver of the bride should ask after the bridegroom's welfare, and ask also his permission to honour him, and upon receiving his answer should honour him by the offer of water for his feet and the like, and saying, "I give this to you," let him give the bridegroom the gifts. The water should be given at the feet and the oblation at the head. Articles for the rinsing of the mouth should be offered at the mouth, and then scents, garlands, two pieces of good cloth, beautiful ornaments and gems, and a sacred thread should be given to the bridegroom, The giver should make madhu-parka by mixing together curd, ghee, and honey in a bell-metal cup, and place it in the hand of the bridegroom with the words, "I give you". The bridegroom, after taking it, should place the cup in his left hand, and, dipping the thumb and ring fingers of his right hand into the madhu-parka, should smell it five times, reciting meanwhile the Pranahuti Mantra, and then place the cup on his north. Having offered the madhu-parka, the bridegroom should be made to rinse his mouth.

The giver of the daughter should then, holding durva and akshata, touch the right knee of the bridegroom with his hand, and then, first meditating on Vishnu and saying "Tat Sat," he should mention the name of the month, the paksha, and tithi, and then the names of the gotra and pravara of the bridegroom and his ancestors one by one, from the great-grandfather, beginning with the last, and ending with the father. The bridegroom's name should be in the objective, and the names of the others in the possessive case. Then follow the bride's name and the names of her ancestors, their gotras, etc.; and he should then say: "I honour thee with the object of giving her to thee in Brahma marriage".

The bridegroom should then say: "I am honoured." The giver upon this should say, "Perform the ordained marriage rites," and the bridegroom should then say: "I do it to the best of my knowledge". The bride, adorned with beautiful clothes and jewels, and covered with another piece of cloth, should then be brought and placed in front of the bridegroom. The giver of the bride should once again show his respect to the bridegroom by the present of clothes and ornaments, and join the right hand of the bridegroom with that of the bride. He should place in their joined hands five gems or a fruit and a pan-leaf, and, having saluted the bride, should consign her to his hands. At the time of consigning the bride the giver should, as before, mention his name twice in the nominative case, and should state his wish, and should also mention the names of the three ancestors of the bridegroom, with their gotras, all in the possessive case, as before.

He should then mention the name of the bridegroom in the dative singular, and then the names of the three ancestors of the bride, with their gotras, etc., in the possessive case. At the time of mentioning the bride's name in the objective singular he should say after that, "The honoured, adorned, clothed, and Prajapati-devataka," and saying, "to thee I give," he should give away the bride. The bridegroom should, saying "Svasti," agree to take her as his wife. Let the giver then say, "In Dharmma, in Artha, in Kama, thou should be with thy wife;" and the bridegroom should reply, saying, "So I shall," and then recite the praise of Kama.

Mantra

It is Kama who gives and Kama who accepts. It is Kama who has taken the Kamini for the satisfaction of Kama. Prompted by Kama, I take thee. May both our kamas be fulfilled.

The giver should then, addressing the son-in-law and the daughter, say: "May, by the grace of Prajapati, the desires of you both be accomplished. May you two fare well. Do you two together perform the religious observances". Then both the bride and bridegroom, to the accompaniment of music and blowing of conch-shells, should be covered with the cloth, so that they may have their first auspicious glance at one another.

Then gold and jewels, according to the giver's means, should be offered to the son-in-law as presents. The giver should then think to himself that the ceremony has been faultlessly done. The bridegroom either, on the same night or the day following, should establish fire, according to the rules of Kushandika.

The fire that is made in this Kushandika is called Yojaka, and the charu which is cooked is called Prajapatya. After performing Dhara Homa in the fire, the bridegroom should offer five oblations. The oblation should, after meditation upon Shiva, Durga, Brahma, Vishnu, and the Carrier of Thunder, be made to them one after the other singly in the sanctified fire. Taking both his wife's hands, the husband should say: "I take thy hands, O fortunate one! Do thou be devoted to the Guru and the Devatas, and duly perform thy household duties according to the religious precepts". The wife should then, with ghee given by the husband, and fried paddy given by her brother, make four oblations in the name of Prajapati. The husband should then rise from his seat with his wife and go round the Fire with her and offer oblations to Durga and Shiva, Rama and Vishnu, Brahmi and Brahma, three times to each couple.

Then, without reciting any Mantra, the bride should step on a stone, and, standing thereon, the bride should take seven steps. If the Kushamdika ceremony is performed at night, the bride and bridegroom, surrounded by the ladies present, should gaze upon the stars Dhruva and Arundhati. Returning to their seats and seated thereon, the bridegroom should bring the ceremony to a close by performing Svishti-krit Homa and offering complete oblations. The Brahma marriage, according to kula-dharmma, in order to be faultless, should take place with a girl of the same caste as the husband, but she should not be of the same gotra, nor should she be a sapinda. The wife married according to Brahma rites is the mistress of the house, and without her permission another wife should not be married according to those rites. O Kuleshvari! if the children of the Brahma wife are living or any of her descendants be living, then the children of the Shaiva wife shall not inherit.

O Parameshvari! the Shaiva wife and her children are entitled to food and clothing from the heir of her Shaiva husband in proportion to the property of the latter. Shaiva marriage celebrated in the Chakra is of two kinds. One kind is terminated with the Chakra and the other is lifelong. At the time of the formation of the Chakra the Vira, surrounded by his friends, relatives, and fellow-worshippers, should, with a well-controlled mind, by mutual consent, perform the marriage ceremony. He should first of all submit their wishes, saying to the Bhairavis and Viras there assembled, "Approve our marriage according to Shaiva form". The Vira should, after obtaining their permission, bow to the Supreme Kalika, repeating the Mantra of seven letters (Kalika Mantra) one hundred and eight times.

O Shiva! he should then say to the woman: "Dost thou love me as thy husband with a guileless heart?".

O Queen of the Devas! the Kaula woman should then honour her beloved with scents, flowers, and coloured rice, and with a faithful heart place her own hands on his. The Lord of the Chakra should then sprinkle them with the following Mantra, and the Kaulas, seated in the Chakra, should approve and say: "It is well"

Mantra

May Raja-rajeshvari, Kali, Tarini, Bhuvaneshvari, Bagala, Kamala, Nitya, Bhairavi, ever protect thee both.

The Lord of the Chakra should sprinkle them twelve times with wine or water of oblation, reciting the above Mantra. The two should then bow to him, and he should upon that let them hear the Vijas of Vagbhava and Rama. There is no restriction of caste or age in Shaiva marriage. By the command of Shambhu, any woman who is not a sapinda, and has not already a husband, may be married.

The wife married for the purposes of Chakra in the Shaiva form should, in the case of the Vira who desires offspring, be released on the dissolution of the Chakra only after the appearance of her menses. The offspring of the Shaiva marriage is of the same caste as the mother if it be an Anuloma marriage, and a Samanya if the marriage is Viloma.

These mixed castes should, at the time of their fathers' shraddha and other ceremonies, give presents of edibles to, and feast the Kaulas only.

Eating and sexual union, O Devi! are desired by, and natural to, men, and their use is regulated for their benefit in the ordinances of Shiva. Therefore, O Mahe-shani! he who follows the ordinances of Shiva undoubtedly acquires Dharmma, Artha, Kama, and Moksha.

End of the Ninth Joyful Message, entitled "The Ten Kinds of Purificatory Rites (Sangskara)."

Chapter 10

Rites relating to Vriddhi Shraddha, Funeral Rites, and Purnabhisheka

SHRI DEVI said:

I have now learned from Thee, O Lord! of the ordinances relating to Kushandika and the ten Sang-skaras. Do Thou now,O Deva! reveal to Me the ordinances relating to Briddhi Shraddha. O Shangkara! tell Me in detail, both for My pleasure and the benefit of all beings, in which of the sacramental and dedicatory ceremonies Kushandika and Briddhi Shraddha should be, or be not, performed. Say this, O Maheshana.

Shri Sadashiva said:

O Gentle One! I have already in detail spoken of all that should be done in the ten Sangskaras commencing from Jiva-seka and ending in marriage, and of all that which should be performed by wise men who desire their own weal.O Beauteous One! I will now speak of what should be done in other rites. Do Thou listen to it.

My Beloved! in consecrating tanks, wells, and ponds, images of Devatas houses, gardens and in vrata, the five Devas and the celestial Mothers should be worshipped, and the Vasu-dhara should be made and Briddhi Shraddha and Kushandika should be performed. In ceremonies which may be, and are, performed by women alone there is no Briddhi Shraddha, but (in lieu thereof) a present of edibles should be made for the satisfaction of the Devatas and the Pitris.

O Lotus-faced One! in such ceremonies the worship of the Deva, Vasu-dhara, and Kushandika should be devoutly performed by the women through the aid of priests. If a man cannot perform a rite himself, then his son, the son's son, the daughter's son, agnate relatives, sister's son and son-in-law and the priest, are, O Shiva! the best substitutes. I will, O Kalika! now in detail speak of Briddhi Shraddha. Do Thou listen to it.

After performing the daily duties, a man should with mind intent worship Ganga, Vishnu–the Lord of Sacrifice, the Divinity of the

110

homestead, and the King; and inwardly reciting the Pranava, he should make nine, seven, five, or three Brahmanas of Darbha grass. The Brahmanas should be made with ends of the grass which have no knots in them, by twisting the upper ends of the blades from right to left two and a half times.

In Briddhi Shraddha and Parvana Shraddha there should be six Brahmanas, but, O Shiva! in Ekoddishta Shraddha there should be only one. The wise one should place the Brahmanas made of kusha grass all in one receptacle, with their faces to the north, and bathe them with the following

Mantra

May the Divinity of water, who is like the Maya Vija, be propitious for the attainment of our desire. May He be propitious in that which we drink, May He always stand forward for our good.

Then with scents and flowers the Brahmanas made with kusha grass should be worshipped. The wise one should then place on the west and the south six vessels in pairs with kusha, sesamum-seed, and Tulasi. On the two vessels placed on the west two of the Brahmanas should be seated facing east, and on the four seats on the south the four Brahmanas should be seated facing north.

The Divinities should be imagined to be in the two seated on the west and the paternal Ancestors in the two seated on the left of those on the south and the maternal ancestors on the right. Know this, O Parvati.

In Abhyudayika Shraddha the Nandimukha fathers and the Nandimukhi mothers, as also the maternal Ancestors in the male line and in the female line, should be mentioned by name. Before this, however, one should turn to his right and face the north, and after the performance of the requisite ceremonies for the worship of the Devas he should turn to his left and face the south and perform the rites necessary for the offering of the Pindas.

In this Abhyudayika Shraddha, O Shiva! all the rites should be performed in their order, beginning with the rites relating to the Devas, and if there be any deviation the Shraddha fails in its object.

The word of supplication addressed to the Devas should be said whilst facing the north, and when the same is addressed to the paternal or maternal Ancestors it should be said whilst facing south. And now, O Thou of pure Smiles! I will first state the words of entreaty which should be addressed to the Devas.

After mentioning the name of the month and paksha, the tithi and the occasion, the excellent worshipper should say "for the prosperous result of the ceremony." Then he should repeat the names and gotras of the three fathers and of the three mothers, and of the three maternal grandfathers and of the three maternal grandmothers, in the possessive case, and he should thereafter say: "I am performing the Shraddha of the Vishva-Devas represented by the image of the two Brahmanas made of kusha grass." These, O Great Devi! are the words of entreaty".

O Parvati! when the Anujna-vakya is either for paternal or maternal Ancestors, the same words should, with the necessary alterations, be said for the paternal and maternal Ancestors, and the Vishva-Devas left out. Then, O Shiva! the worshipper should recite the Brahma-Vidya Gayatri ten times. He should next say the following

Mantra

The excellent worshipper, having repeated the above Mantra three times, and taking water in his hand, should wash the Shraddha articles with the

Mantra

Vang, Hung, Phat.

O Mistress of the Kula! a vessel should next be placed in the corner of Agni. Then uttering the

Mantra

O Water! Thou art the nectar which killest the Rakshasas, protect this sacrifice of mine.

Water with Tulasi-leaves and barley should be put into it; and the wise one should, after first offering handfuls of water to the Devas and then to the Vipras, give them seats of kusha grass.

The learned men, O Shiva! should then invoke the Vishva-Devas, the fathers, the mothers, the maternal grandfathers, and the maternal grandmothers. Having so invoked them, the Vishva-Devas should first be worshipped; and then the three fathers, the three mothers, the three maternal grandfathers, and the three maternal grandmothers should be worshipped, with offets of Padya, Arghya, Achamaniya, incense, lights, cloths. Then, O Beauteous One! permission should be asked in the first place of the Devas for the spreading of the leaves.

Then a four-sided figure should be drawn uttering the Maya Vija, and then in a similar way for the paternal and maternal sides two figures each should be drawn. After these have been sprinkled with the Varuna Vija, leaves should be spread over the figures. These leaves should be sprinkled with the Varuna Vija, and then drinking-water and different kinds of edibles and rice should be distributed in their order.

112

After giving honey and grains of barley and sprinkling the offerings with water, accompanied by the

Mantra

Hrang, Hrung, Phat,

the worshipper possessed of the knowledge of Truth should dedicate the edibles by the names of the Vishva-Devas, the fathers, the mothers, the maternal grandfathers and the maternal grandmothers, and thereafter repeat the Gayatri ten times and thrice repeat the

Mantra

"I salute the Divinities," as aforesaid.

After this, O Adya! he should take the directions (of the officiating Brahmanas) relating to the disposal of the remnants of edibles and of the Pindas.

Upon receiving the directions of the Brahmana, he should, O Beloved! make twelve Pindas of the size of bael fruits with the remnants of the Akshata and other things. He should make one more Pinda equal in size with the others, and then, O Ambika! he should spread some kusha grass and barley on the Nairrita corner of the figure.

Mantra

Such of my family as have none to offer Pindas to them whom neither son nor wife survive, who were burnt to death or were killed by tigers or other beast of prey, such kinsmen of mine as themselves are without kinsmen, all such as were my kinsmen in previous births, may they all obtain imperishable satisfaction by the Pinda and water hereby given by me.

O Adored of the Devas! having with the above Mantra offered the Pinda to those who have no one to offer them Pindas, he should wash his hands and inwardly recite the Gayatri, and repeat the

Mantra

"I salute the Divinities,"

and so forth, three times, and then make the square.

O Devi! the wise man should in front of the vessels containing the remnants of the offerings make such squares in twos (for his Ancestors), beginning with the paternal Ancestors.

O Shive! he should then sprinkle the squares with water with the Mantra already prescribed, and then spread kusha grass over them and sprinkle them with the Vayu Vija, beginning with the kusha spread on the square for the paternal (male) Ancestors, and then offer three Pindas, one at the top, another at the bottom, and one in the middle, in each of the squares.

O Maheshvari! the names of each of the Ancestors should be mentioned, inviting him or her, and then the Pinda should be given with honey and barley, concluding with Svadha. After the Pindas are given (in manner aforesaid) the Lepa-bhoji Ancestors should be satisfied by the offer to them of the remnants which remain on the hand. These should be scattered on all sides with the

Mantra

Ong, may the Lepa-bhoji Ancestors be pleased.

In Ekoddishta Shraddha the offering to the Lepa-bhoji Ancestors is not made.

Then for the satisfaction of the Devas and Pitris the Gayatri should be inwardly recited ten times, and the Mantra, "I salute the Divinities," as aforesaid should be similarly recited three times, and then the Pindas should be worshipped. Lighting an incense-stick and a light, the wise one should, with closed eyes, think of the Pitris in their celestial forms partaking of their allotted Pindas, each his own, and should then bow to them, uttering the following

Mantra

My father is my highest Dharmma. My father is my highest Tapas. My father is my Heaven. On my father being satisfied, the whole Universe is satisfied.

Taking up some flowers from the remnants, the Pitris should be asked for their blessings, with the following

Mantra

Give me your blessings, O Merciful Pitris. May my knowledge, progeny, and kinsmen always increase. May my benefactors prosper. May I have food in profusion. May many always beg of me, and may I not have to beg of any.

Then he should remove the Devas and Brahmanas made of kusha grass, as also the Pindas, commencing with the Devas. The wise one should then make presents to all three.

He should then make japa of the Gayatri ten times, and the Mantra, "I salute the Divinities," five times, and, after looking at the fire and the Sun, should, with folded palms, ask the Vipra the following question:

"Is the Shraddha complete?" and the Brahmana should make reply:

"It has been completed according to the injunctions".

Then, for the removal of the effects of any error or omission, the Pranava should be inwardly recited ten times, and the ceremony should be brought to a close, uttering the following

Mantra

"May the Shraddha rite be faultless";

And then the food and drink in the vessels should be offered to the officiating Brahmana.

In the absence of a Vipra, it should be given to cows and goats, or should be thrown into water. This is called "Vriddhi Shraddha," enjoined for all obligatory sacramental rites. Shraddha performed on the occasion of any Parvvan is called "Parvvana Shraddha".

In ceremonies relating to the consecration of emblems or images of Devas, or while starting for or returning from pilgrimage, the Shraddha should be according to the injunctions laid down for Parvvana Shraddha. On the occasion of Parvvana Shraddha the Pitris should not be addressed with the prefix "Nandimukha," and for the words "Salutation to Pushti" should be substituted the words "Salutation to Svadha".

O Beautiful One! if any of the three Ancestors be alive, then the wise one should make the offerings to another Ancestor of higher degree. If the father, grandfather, and great-grandfather be alive, then, O Queen of the Devas! no Shraddha need be performed. If they are pleased, then the object of the funeral rite and sacrifice is attained.

If his father be living, then a man may perform his mother's Shraddha, his wife's Shraddha, and Nandi-mukha Shraddha; but he is not entitled to perform the Shraddha of anyone else.O Queen of the Kula! at the time of Ekoddishta Shraddha the Vishva-Devas are not to be worshipped. The word of entreaty should be addressed to one Ancestor only.

At the time of Ekoddishta Shraddha cooked rice and Pinda should be given whilst facing south. The rest of the ceremony is the same as that which has been already described, with the exception that sesamum should be substituted for barley.

The peculiarity in Preta Shraddha is that the worship of Ganga and others is omitted, and in the framing of the Mantra the deceased should be spoken of as Preta whilst rice and Pindas are offered to him.

The Shraddha performed for one man is called "Ekoddishta." In offering Pinda to the Preta, fish and meat should be added. O Mistress of the Kula! know this, that the Shraddha which is performed on the day following the end of the period of uncleanliness is Preta Shraddha. If there is a miscarriage, or if the child dies immediately on birth, or if a child is born or dies, then the period of uncleanliness is to be reckoned according to the custom of the family.

The period of uncleanliness in the case of the twice-born is ten days (for Brahmanas), twelve (for Kshatriyas), and a fortnight (for Vaishyas); for Shudras and Samanyas the period is one month (thirty days).

On the death of an Agnate who is not a Sapinda, the period of uncleanliness is three days, and on the death of a Sapinda, should information of it arrive after the period prescribed, one becomes unclean for three days.

The unclean man, O Primordial One! is not entitled to perform any rite relating to the Devas and the Pitris, excepting Kula worship and that which has been already commenced.

Persons over five years of age should be burnt in the burning-ground, but, O Kuleshani! a wife should not be burnt with her dead husband. Every woman is Thy image—Thou residest concealed in the forms of all women in this world. That woman who in her delusion ascends the funeral pyre of her lord shall go to hell.

Kalika! the corpses of worshippers of Brahman should be either buried, thrown into running water, or burnt, according as they may direct.

Ambika! death in a holy place or a place of pilgrimage, or near the Devi, or near the Kaulikas, is a happy one.

He who at the time of his death meditates on the one Truth, forgetful of the three worlds, attains to his own Essential Being.

After death the corpse should be taken to the burning-ground, and when it has been washed it should be smeared with ghee and placed on the pyre, with the face to the north.

The deceased should be addressed by his name, and Gotra and as Preta. Giving the Pinda to the mouth of the corpse, the pyre should be lighted by applying the torch to the mouth of the corpse, inwardly the while reciting the Vahni Vija.

Beloved! the Pinda should be made of boiled or unboiled rice, or crushed barley, or wheat, and should be of the size of an emblic myrobalam. To the eldest son of the Preta is given the privilege of performing the Shraddha; in his absence to the other sons, according to the order of their seniority.

The day after the day upon which the period of uncleanliness expires, the mourner should bathe and purify himself, and give away gold and sesamum for the liberation of the Preta.

The son of the Preta should give away cattle, lands, clothes, carriages, vessels made of metals, and various kinds of edibles, in order that the Preta may attain Heaven.

He should also give away scents, garlands, fruits, water, a beautiful bed, and everything which the Preta himself liked to insure his passage to Heaven.

Then a bull should be branded with the mark of a trident, and decorated with gold and ornaments, and then let loose, with the object that the deceased may attain Heaven.

He should then with a devout spirit perform the Shraddha, according to the injunctions laid down for the performance of Preta Shraddha, and then feed Brahmanas and Kaulas possessed of Divine knowledge, and the hungry.

The man who is unable to make gifts should perform the Shraddha to the best of his ability, and feed the hungry, and thus liberate his father from the state of existence of a Preta.

This Preta Shraddha is known as Adya or Ekod-dishta Shraddha, and it liberates the deceased from the state of Preta. After this every year on the tithi of his death edibles should be given to the deceased.

There is no necessity for a multitude of injunctions nor for a multitude of rituals. Man may attain all siddhi by honouring a Kaulika. The object of all Sangskaras is completely attained if, in lieu of the prescribed Homa, Japa, and Shraddha, even a single Kaulika is duly honoured, at the time of the ceremony.

The injunction of Shiva is that all auspicious ceremonies should be performed between the period beginning with the fourth day of the light half of the lunar half-month, and ending on the fifth of the dark half-month.

He, however, who is desirous of performing any rite which must be performed may perform it even on an inauspicious day, provided he be so directed by his Guru, by a Ritvij, or a Kaulika.

A Kaulika should commence the building of a house, should first enter a house, start on a journey, wear new jewels, and the like, only after worshipping the Primordial One with the five Elements.

Or the excellent worshipper may shorten the rite. He may thus, after meditating on the Devi, and inwardly reciting the Mantra and bowing to the Devi, go wherever he may desire.

In the worship of all Devatas, such as the Autumnal Festival and others, dhyana and puja should be performed according to the ordinances laid down in the Shastras relating to such worship.

According to the ordinances relating to the worship of the Primordial Kali, animal sacrifice and Homa should be performed, and the rite should be brought to an end by the honouring of Kaulikas and making of offerings.

The Kaulika is the most excellent Dharmma, the Kaulika is the most excellent Deva, the Kaulika is the most excellent pilgrimage, therefore should the Kaula be always worshipped.

The three and a half kotis of Places of Pilgrimage, all the Devas beginning with Brahma Himself, reside in the body of the Kaula. What, therefore, is there which is not attained by worshipping him? The land in which the good and fully initiated Kaula resides is blessed and deserving of honour. It is most holy, and is coveted even by the Devas. Who can in this world understand the majesty of the fully initiated Sadhaka, who is Shiva Himself, and to whom there is nothing either holy or sinful?.

Such a Kaula, possessing merely the form of man, moves about this earth for the salvation of the entire world and the instruction of men in the conduct of life.

Shri Devi said:

Thou hast, O Lord! spoken of the greatness of the Soul of the fully initiated Kaula. Do Thou in Thy mercy speak to Me of the ordinances relating to such initiation.

Shri Sadashiva said:

In the three Ages this rite was a great secret.; men then used to perform it in all secrecy, and thus attain liberation.

When the Kali Age prevails, the followers of Kula rite should declare themselves as such, and, whether in the night or the day, should openly be initiated.

By the mere drinking of wine, without initiation, a man does not become a Kaula. The Kula worshipper becomes the Lord of the Kula Chakra only after full initiation.

The Guru should, the day before the initiation, worship the Deva of Obstacles with offerings, according to his ability for the removal of all obstacles.

Adding successively six long vowels to the Mula Mantra, Shadanga-nyasa should be performed, and O Shiva! after doing Pranayama let Ganapati be meditated upon.

Dhyana

Meditate on Gana-pati as of the colour of vermilion, having three eyes, a large belly, holding in His lotus-hands the conch, the noose, the elephant-goad, and the sign of blessing. His great trunk adorned with the jar of wine which it holds. On His forehead shines the young Moon. He has the head of the King of elephants; His cheeks are constantly bathed in wine. His hody is adorned with the coils of the King of servants. He is dressed in red raiment, and His body is smeared with scented ointments.

Having thus meditated upon Ganapati, he should be worshipped with mental offerings, and then the protecting power of the seat should be worshipped. These are Tibra, Jvalini, Nanda, Bhoga-da, Kama-rupini, Ugra, Tejasvati, Satyi, and Vighna-vinashini. The first eight should be worshipped in their order, beginning from the east, and the last should be worshipped in the middle of the Mandala. Having thus worshipped them all, the lotus-seat itself should be worshipped.

Meditating on Ganesha once again, He should be worshipped with offerings of the five elements. On each of His four sides should the excellent Kaulika worship Ganesha, Gana-nayaka, Gana-natha, Gana-krida, Eka-danta, Rakta-tunda, Lambodara, Gajanana, Mahodara, Vikata, Dhumrabha, and Vighna-nashana.

Then the eight Shaktis, Brahmi, and others, and the ten Dikpalas and their weapons, should be worshipped, and after that Vighna-raja should be bidden to depart.

Having thus worshipped the King of Obstacles, the worshipper should perform the preliminary ceremony, and then entertain the Kaulas versed in divine knowledge with the five elements.

The next day, having bathed and performed his ordinary daily duties as already enjoined, he should, O Beloved! give away sesamum-seed and gold for the destruction of all sins from his birth, and a bhojya for the satisfaction of the Kaulas. Then, giving arghya to Suryya, and having worshipped Brahma, Vishnu, Shiva, and the nine Planets, as also the sixteen divine Mothers, he should make a Vasu-dhara.

He should then perform Vriddhi Shraddha for the good result of the rite, and, going up to the Guru, bow to him, and pray to him as follows:

(Prayer to the Guru)

Save me, O Lord! thou that art the Sun of the Kaulas. Protect my head, O Ocean of Mercy! with the shade of thy lotus-foot. Grant us leave, O Exalted One! in this auspicious Purnabhisheka that by thy grace I may attain the success of my undertaking without any hindrance.

(The Guru should then reply:)

My son! be thou, by the permission of the Shiva-Shakti, initiated with the full initiation. May thou attain the object of thy desire by the command of Shiva.

Having thus obtained the permission of the spiritual Preceptor, he should make the Sangkalpa for the removal of all obstacles and for the attainment of long life, prosperity, strength, and good health.

The Sadhaka, having solemnly formed his resolve, should worship the Guru, by presenting him with clothes and jewels, and karana with Shuddhi, and do honour to him.

The Guru should then make with earth an altar four fingers in height and measuring one and a half cubit either way in a beautiful room painted with red earth, etc., decorated with pictures, flags, fruits, and leaves, and strings of small bells.

The room should have a beautiful ceiling-cloth, lighted with lines of lamps fed with ghee to dispel all traces of darkness, and should be scented with burning camphor, incense-sticks, and incense, and ornamented with fans, fly-whisks, the tail feathers of the peacock, and mirrors, etc., and then he should with rice powdered and coloured yellow, red, black, white, and dark blue draw Mandala called Sarvato-bhadra, beautiful and auspicious in every way.

Then each person should perform the rite preparatory to mental worship, according to his Sangkalpa, and then, having made mental worship, should purify the five elements with the Mantra previously mentioned. After the Pancha-tattvas have been purified, the jar, which must be either of gold or silver or copper or earth, should be placed with the Brahma Vija on the Mandala. It should be washed with the Weapon Mantra and smeared with curd, Akshata, and then a vermilion mark should be placed on it with the Mantra "Shring".

120

He should then recite three times the letters of the alphabet, with the Vindu superposed from Ksha to A, and recite inwardly the Mula Mantra, and fill the jar with wine or water from some holy place, or with ordinary pure water, and then throw into the jar nine gems or gold.

The merciful Guru should then place over the mouth of the jar a leafy branch of a Jack-tree, a Fig-tree, an Ashvattha-tree, and of a Vakula and Mango-tree, with the Vagbhava Vija.

He should then place on the leafy branch a gold, silver, copper, or earthen platter, uttering the Rama Vija and Maya Vija. Then, O Beauteous One! two pieces of cloth should be tied to the neck of the jar. When worshipping Shakti the cloth should be of a red colour, and in the worship of Shiva and Vishnu it should be white.

Inwardly reciting the

Mantra

Sthang, Sthing, Hring, Shring,

the jar should be fixed in its place, and after putting into it the Pancha-tattvas the nine cups should be placed in their order. The Shakti Patra should be of silver, the Guru Patra of gold, the Shri Patra should be made of the human skull, the rest of copper. Cups made of stone, wood, and iron should be rejected; the material of the cups in the worship of the Maha-Devi should be according to the means of the worshipper.

After placing the cups, libations should be offered to the four Gurus and the Devi, and the wise one should then worship the jar filled with nectar. Lights and incense should then be waved and sacrifices made to all beings, and after worshipping the divinities of the pitha he should perform Shadangganyasa. He should then do Pranayama, and, meditating on the Great Devi, invoke Her, and thereafter worship Her, the Object of his worship, to the best of his ability and without niggardliness. The excellent Guru, O Shiva! should perform all the rites ending with Homa, and then honour the Kumaris and worshippers of Shakti by presenting them with flowers, sandal-paste, and clothes.

The Guru should then ask the permission of those present with the following words:

O you Kaulas! who are vowed to Kula-worship, be kind to my disciple. Do you give your permission to his Sangskara of Purnabhisheka.

The Lord of the Chakra, having thus asked those present, should respectfully say: "By the grace of Mahamaya and the majesty of the Supreme Soul, may thy disciple be perfect and devoted to the Supreme Essence".

The Guru should then make the disciple worship the Devi in the jar, which has been worshipped by himself, and then, mentally repeating the

Mantra

Kling, Hring, Shring

over it, move the immaculate jar, with the following

Mantra

Rise, O Brahma-kalasha, thou art the Devata and grantest all success. May my disciple, being bathed with thy water and leaves, be devoted to Brahman.

Having moved the jar in this manner, the Guru should mercifully sprinkle the disciple seated with his face to the North with the Mantra about to be spoken.

Mantra

May the Gurus sprinkle thee. May Brahma, Vishnu, and Maheshvara sprinkle thee; may the Mothers Durga, Lakshmi, Bhavani, sprinkle thee; may Shodashi, Tarini, Nitya, Svaha, Mahisha-mardini, all these sprinkle thee with the water that has been sanctified by the Mantra; may Jaya-durga, Vishalakshi, Brahmani, Sarasvati, may all These sprinkle thee; may Bagala, Varada, and Shiva sprinkle thee; may the Shaktis, Narasinghi, Varahi, Vaishnavi, Vana-malini, Indrani, Varuni, Raudri, sprinkle thee; may Bhairavi, Bhadra-kali, Tushti, Pushti, Uma, Kshama, Shraddha, Kanti, Daya, Shanti, always sprinkle thee; may Maha-kali, Maha-lakshmi, Maha-nila-sarasvati, Ugra-chanda, Prachanda, constantly sprinkle thee; may Matsya, Kurma, Varaha, Nrisingha, Vamana, Rama, Bhrigu-Rama, sprinkle thee with water; may Asitanga, Ruru, Chanda, Krodhonmatta, Bhayangkara, Kapali, Bhishana, sprinkle thee; may Kali, Kapalini, Kulla, Kurukulla, Virodhini, Viprachitta, Mahogra, ever sprinkle thee; may Indra, Agni, Shamana, Raksha, Varuna, Pavana, Dhana-da, Maheshana, who are the eight Dikpalas, sprinkle thee; may Ravi, Soma, Mangala, Budha, Jiva, Sita, Shani, Rahu, Ketu, with all their Satellites, sprinkle thee; may the stars, the Karanas, the Yogas, the Days of the Week, and the two Divisions of the Month, the Days, Seasons, Months, and the Year anoint thee always; may the Salt Ocean, the Sweet Ocean, the Ocean of Wine, the Ocean of Ghee, the Ocean of Curd, the Ocean of Milk, the Ocean of Sweet Water sprinkle thee with their consecrated waters; may Ganga, Yamuna, Reva, Chandra-bhaga, Sarasvati, Sarayu, Gandaki, Kunti, Shveta-ganga, Kaushiki, may all these sprinkle thee with their consecrated waters; may the great Nagas beginning with Ananta, the birds beginning with Garuda, the trees beginning with the Kalpa tree, and the great Mountains sprinkle thee; may the beneficent Beings residing in Patala, on the earth, and in the air, pleased at this hour of thy Purnabhisheka, sprinkle thee with water. May thy ill-luck, bad name, illness, melancholy and sorrows be destroyed by the Purnabhisheka, and by the glory of the Supreme Brahman. May Alakshmi, Kala-karni, the Dakinis, and the Yoginis, being driven away by the Kali Vija, be destroyed by the Abhisheka. May the Bhuta, Preta, Pishachas, and the maleficent Planets be driven out, put to flight, and destroyed by the Rama Vija; may all misfortune caused thee by magic and by the incantations of thy enemies, may all thy transgressions of mind, word, and body be destroyed as the result of this initiation; may all thy adversities be destroyed, may thy prosperity be undisturbed, may all thy desires be fulfilled as the result of this Purnabhisheka.

With these twenty-one Mantras the disciple should be sprinkled with water; and if he has obtained already the Mantra from the mouth of a Pashu, the Guru should make him hear it again.

The Kaulika Guru should, having informed the worshippers of Shakti, call his disciple by his name and give him a name ending with Anandanatha.

Being thus initiated in the Mantra by the Guru, the disciple should worship his Ishta-devata in the Yantra (of the Guru), and then honour the Guru by presenting him with the Pancha-tattvas.

The disciple should also give as Dakshina cows, land, gold, clothes, drinks, and jewels to the Guru, and then honour the Kaulas, who are the very embodiments of Shiva.

The self-possessed, purified, and humble disciple, having honoured the Kaulas, should touch the sacred feet of the Guru with veneration, and, bowing to him, pray to him as follows:

Prayer to Guru

Holy Lord! Thou art the Lord of the world. Lord! thou art my Lord. O Ocean of Mercy! do Thou gratify my heart's desire by the gift of the excellent nectar.

The Guru should then say:

"Give me leave, O Kaulas! you who are the visible images of Shiva Himself, that I may give to my good and humble disciple the excellent nectar".

The Kaulas will then say:

"Lord of the Chakra! thou art the Supreme Lord Himself, Thou art the Sun of the Kaula lotus. Do Thou gratify this good disciple, and give him the Kaula nectar".

The Guru, having obtained the leave of the Kaulas, should place in the hand of the disciple the drinking-cup filled with the excellent nectar, as also the Shuddhi.

The Guru should then, devoutly meditating on the Devi in his heart, place the tilaka on the forehead of the disciple, as also of the Kaulas, with the ashes adhering to the sacrificial spoon.

Let the Guru then distribute the Tattvas offered to the Devi, and partake of the food and drink as directed in the injunctions relating to the formation of Chakra.

O Devi! I have spoken to Thee of the auspicious rites relating to Purnabhisheka. By this one attains divine knowledge and becomes Shiva Himself.

The Purnabhisheka should be performed for nine or seven or five or three or one night.

There are, O Kuleshani! five different forms in this purificatory rite. In the rite which lasts nine nights the Mandala known as Sarvato-bhadra should be made.

Beloved! in the rite which lasts seven nights the Mandala Nava-nabha, in the rite which lasts five nights the Mandala Panchabja, in the rite which lasts three nights and in the rite which lasts one night the Mandala of eight-petalled lotus should be respectively made.

O Devi! the injunction is that on the Sarvato-bhadra and Nava-nabha Mandalas nine jars should be placed, on Panchabja Mandala five, and on Ashta-dalabja Mandala one jar, and the Angga-Devatas and the Avarana-Devatas should be worshipped in the filaments and other parts of the lotuses.

The Kaulas who have been fully initiated are pure of soul. All things are purified by their looking, touching, and by their smelling them. All men, whether they are Shaktas, Vaishnavas, Shaivas, Sauras, or Ganapatas, should worship the Kaula Sadhu with devotion.

It is good for a Shakta to have a Guru who is a Shakta, for a Shaiva a Shaiva Guru is commendable, and for a Vaishnava a Vaishnava, for a Saura a Saura as Guru is advised, and a Ganapata is the proper Guru for a Ganapata, but a Kaula is excellent as Guru in the case of all; therefore the wise one should with all his soul be initiated by a Kaula. Those who worship the Kaulas with Pancha-tattva and with heart uplifted cause the salvation of their Ancestors, and themselves attain the highest end.

The man who has obtained the Mantra from the mouth of a Pashu is of a certainty a Pashu, and he who has obtained the Mantra from a Vira is a Vira, and he who obtains it from a Kaula knows the Brahman. One who has been initiated according to Shakta rites is a Vira; he may purify the Pancha-tattvas only in the worship of his own Ishta-devata, he may never be the Chakreshvara.

He who kills a Vira, he who drinks wine which has not been consecrated, he who seduces the wife of or steals the property of a Vira, these four are great sinners, and the man who associates with any of these is the fifth sinner. Those evil-natured men who disparage the Kula Way, Kula articles, and the Kula worshipper go down the low and vile path.

The Rudra-dakinis and Rudra-bhairavis dance in joy (at the thought of) chewing the bones and flesh of men who hate wine and the Kaulas. They are merciful and truthful, and ever desire the good of others, for such as slander them there is no escape from Hell.

I have in the various Tantras spoken of various ceremonies and of many repetitions of practices; but in the case of a Kaula who is devoted to the Brahman, it is a matter of indifference whether he practises or omits them.

There is one Supreme Brahman Who exists, spread throughout the Universe (or any part of it). He is worshipped, because there is nothing which exists apart from Him.

Beloved! even those who look to the fruit of action and are governed by their desires and by the worship of different Devas, and addicted to worldly pursuits, go to and become united with Him. He who sees everything in Brahman, and who sees Brahman everywhere, is undoubtedly known as an excellent Kaula, who has attained liberation while yet living.

End of the Tenth Joyful Message, entitled "Rites relating to Vriddhi Shraddha, Funeral Rites, and Purnabhisheka."

Chapter 11

The Account of Expiatory Rites

LISTENING to the injunctions of Shambhu relating to the different castes and stages of life, Aparna was greatly pleased, and questioned Shangkara thus:

Shri Devi said:

Thou hast, O Lord! out of Thy kindness for Me and in Thy omniscience, spoken of the customs and the rules of religious conduct and sacraments for the well-being of the world. But the men of the Kali Age, being wicked, and blinded by anger and lust, atheists, of wavering minds and addicted to the gratification of their senses, will not in their ignorance and folly follow the way laid down by Thee; it behoves Thee, O Ishana! to say what will be the means of their liberation.

Shri Sadashiva said:

Thou hast asked well, O Devi! Thou who art the Benefactress of the world, the Mother of the world, Thou art Durga, Thou liberatest people from the bonds of birth and the toils of this world. Thou art the Primordial One, Thou fosterest and guardest this world, Thou art beyond the most excellent; Thou, O Devi! supportest the moving and the motionless Universe. Thou art Earth, Thou art Water, Thou art Fire, Thou art Air,

Thou art the Void, Thou art consciousness itself, Thou art the mahat-tattva. Thou art life in this world;

Thou art the knowledge of self, and Thou art the Supreme Divinity. Thou art the senses; Thou art the mind, Thou art the intellect; Thou art the motion and existence of the Universe.

Thou art the Vedas, Thou art the Pranava, Thou art the Smritis, the Sanghitas, the Nigamas, the Agamas, and the Tantras, Thou pervadest all the Shastras, and art the Abode of all that is good. Thou art Mahakali,

Mahalakshmi, Maha-nila-sarasvati, Mahodari, Mahamaya, Maharaudri, and Maheshvari; Thou art Omniscient and full of knowledge, there is nothing which Thou knowest not; yet, O Wise One! since Thou askest Me, I will speak of it for Thy pleasure.

Thou hast truly spoken, O Devi! of the ways of men, who, knowing what is for their welfare, yet, maddened by sinful desire for things which bring immediate enjoyment, and devoid of the sense of right and wrong, will desert the True Path. I speak now of that which will contribute to their salvation.

In the doing of what is forbidden and in the omitting of what is enjoined men sin, and sins lead to pain, sorrow, and disease.

O Kula-nayika! know that there are two kinds of sin – that which contributes merely to the injury of one's own self, and that which causes injury to others. Man is released of the sin of injuring others by the punishment inflicted by the King, and from other sins by expiatory rites and Samadhi.

Those sinful men who are not purified by either punishment or expiation cannot but go to hell, and are despised both in this world and the next.

O Adya! I shall first of all speak of the Rules relating, O Maheshvari! to punishment by the King. The King who deviates from these himself goes upon the downward path.

In the administration of justice, servants, sons, mendicants, friends, and foes should all be treated alike.

If the King is guilty of any sin himself, or if he should have wronged one who is not guilty, then he may purify himself by fasting and by placating those he has wronged by gifts. If the King should consider that he is guilty of any sin which is punishable by death, he should then abdicate his kingdom and go to a forest, and there labour for his liberation and penances. The King should not, without sufficient reason, inflict heavy punishment on persons guilty of a light offence, nor should he inflict light punishment on persons guilty of a great offence. But the punishment by which many offenders may be deterred from ill-doing, and (punishment) in the case of an offender who is fearless of crimes, should be heavy, although the offence be a light one.

In the case of one who has committed the offence but once only and is ashamed of his ill-deed, or of one who fears crime and is a respectable man, a light punishment should be inflicted, even if the offence be a grave one.

If a Kaula or a Brahmana is guilty of a slight offence, they should even, though highly honourable, be punished by the King by a rebuke.

The King who does not bestow adequate rewards and punishments after consultation with his ministers is a great sinner.

A son should not leave his mother and father, the subjects should not leave their King, nor the wife her husband, even though they are greatly guilty.

The subjects should actively protect the kingdom, property, and life of the just King; otherwise they will go upon the downward path.

Shiva! those who knowingly go with their, mother, daughter, or sister, those who have killed their Maha-gurus, those who have, after having taken refuge in the Kula Faith, abandoned it, and those who have broken the trust placed in them, are great sinners.

Shiva! the punishment of those that go with their mother, sister, and daughter is death, and if the latter are wilful participants the same punishment should be inflicted upon them.

The sinful man who with a lustful mind goes to the bed of his mother or father's sister, or daughters-in-law, or mothers-in-law (wife's mother), the wife of his preceptor, the wife of his maternal or paternal grandfather, the daughter or wife of his mother or father's brother, the wife or daughter of his brother, the sister's daughter, the master's wife or daughter, or with an unmarried girl, should be punished by castration, and these women also if they are wilful participants in the crime should be punished by the cutting of their noses and turning them out of the house that they may be released from sin.

The punishment of the man who goes with the wife or daughter of a sapinda, or with the wife of a man who has trusted him, is to be deprived of all his property and to have his head shaved.

If through mistake (by ignorance) one should happen to marry any of these, either in Brahma or Shaiva form, then she should at once be disespoused.

A man who goes with the wife of another man of the same caste as himself, or of a caste inferior to his own, should be punished by the imposition of a fine and by being kept on a diet of grains for one month.

If a Kshatriya, Vaishya, Shudra, or Samanya, O Thou of Beauteous Face! goes with a Brahmana woman knowing her to be such, then his punishment is castration, and the Brahmana woman should be disfigured and banished from his kingdom by the King. For such as go with the wives of Viras, and for such wives, the punishment should be the same.

128

The wicked man who enjoys the wife of one of a higher caste should be heavily fined, and kept on a diet of grains for three months.

And if the woman is a wilful party, she should be punished as above mentioned. If the wife is the victim of a rape, then she should be separated from, but maintained by, her husband.

A wife, whether married according to Brahma or Shaiva form, should in all cases be renounced if she has gone with another even if it be only once, and then whether of her own desire or against it.

Those who have intercourse with public women, or with cows or other animals, should, O Deveshi! be purified by being kept on a diet of grains for three nights.

The punishment of those wicked men who have unnatural intercourse with a woman is death; this is the injunction of Shambhu.

A man who ravishes a woman, even if she be the wife of a Chandala, should be punished by death, and should never be pardoned.

A man should consider as wife only that woman who has been married to him according to Brahma or Shaiva form. All other women are the wives of others.

A man who with lust looks at another man's wife should fast for a day to purify himself. He who accosts her in a secret place should fast for two days. He who touches her should fast for four days; and he who embraces her should fast for eight days to purify himself.

And the woman who with a lustful mind behaves in the same manner should purify herself by following the same rules of fasting.

The man who uses offensive language towards a woman, who sees the private parts of a woman who is not his wife, and laughs derisively at her, should fast for two days to purify himself.

A man who shows his naked body to another, or who makes another person naked, should cease eating for two days to purify himself.

If the husband proves that his wife has had intercourse with another, then the King should punish her and her paramour according to the injunction laid down.

If the husband (has good cause to believe and yet) is unable to prove the faithlessness of his wife, then he should separate from her, but he should maintain her if she remains under his control.

If the husband, on seeing his wife enjoying with her paramour, kills her with her paramour, then the King should not punish him with death.

If the husband prohibits the wife to go to any place or to talk with anyone, then the wife should neither go to that place nor talk with that person.

If, on the death of the husband, the widow lives with the relatives of the husband under their control, following the customs of a widow's life, or in their absence she lives with the relatives of her father, then she deserves to inherit her husband's property.

The widow should not eat twice a day, nor should she eat food cooked by one who is not her husband's Agnate; she should renounce sexual enjoyment, animal food, jewels, sleeping on soft beds, and coloured clothes.

The widow faithful to her Dharmma should not anoint herself with fragrant ointments, she should avoid village gossip, and should spend her time in the worship of the Deities and in the performance of Vratas.

In the case of the boy who has neither father, mother, nor paternal grandfather, the mother's relatives are the best guardians. The mother's mother, mother's father, mother's brother, mother's brother's son, mother's father's brother, these are the relatives on the mother's side.

Father's mother, father, brother, father's brother's and sister's sons, father's father's brother, are known as paternal relatives.

The husband's mother, father, brother, the husband's brother's and sister's sons, and the husband's father's brothers, all these are known as the relatives of the husband.

Ambika! the King should compel a man, according to his means, to give food and clothes to his father, mother, father's father, father's mother, the wife whose son cannot support her, and to the maternal grandfather and grandmother, who are poor and have no son.

If a man speaks rudely to his wife he must fast for a day, if he beats her he must go without food for three days, and if he causes her bloodshed then he must fast for seven days.

If a man in his anger or folly calls his wife his mother, his sister, or daughter, then he should purify himself by fasting seven days.

If a girl be married to an impotent man, then the King should cause her to be married again, even if the fact is discovered after the lapse of some time. This is Shiva's injunction.

If a girl becomes a widow before consummation of marriage, she also ought to be remarried. This also is the command of Shiva.

130

The woman who is delivered of a child within six months of her marriage, or after the lapse of a year following her husband's death, is not a wife, nor is the child legitimate.

The woman who causes a miscarriage before the completion of the fifth month, as well as the person who helps her thereto, should be heavily punished.

The woman who after the fifth month destroys the child in her womb, and the person who helps her thereto, are guilty of killing a human being.

The cruel man who wilfully kills another man should always be sentenced to death by the King.

The King should correct the man who kills another man through ignorance, or in a fit of passion, or by mistake, either by taking his property from him or by giving him a severe beating.

The man who tries to compass his own death, whether by himself or by the aid of another, should be awarded the same punishment as the man who kills another through ignorance.

The man who kills another in a duel, or kills an enemy who attempts to kill him, is not guilty of any offence.

The King should punish the man who has maimed another by maiming him, and the man who has beaten another by having him beaten.

The wicked man who flings any missile, or lifts his hand to strike a Vipra, or one who should be honoured, or who strikes either of them, should be punished by a pecuniary fine for the first offence, and by the burning of his hand for a second offence.

If a man dies consequent upon a wound inflicted by any weapon or otherwise after six months, then the offender should be punished for the assault, and shall not be punished with death by the King.

If the King kills subverters of his government, men who plot to usurp his kingdom, servants secretly befriending the King's enemies, men creating dissatisfaction against the King among the troops, subjects who wish to wage war against the King, or armed highway robbers, he shall not be guilty of any sin.

The man who kills another, compelled by his master's order, is not himself guilty of the killing, for it is the master's killing. This is the command of Shiva.

If a man's death is caused by a beast belonging to, or weapons in the hand of, a careless man, then the latter should be punished by a pecuniary or bodily punishment.

Those detestable persons who disobey the King's command, who are arrogant in their speech in the King's presence, or who decry the Kula faith, should be punished by the King.

He who misappropriates property entrusted to him, the malicious man, the cheat, he who creates ill-feeling between men, or who makes people quarrel with one another, should be banished from the kingdom by the King.

The King should banish from his kingdom those abandoned and wicked-minded men who give away their sons and daughters in marriage for money, and who give their daughters (in marriage) to impotent husbands.

Persons who attempt to harm others by the spreading of baseless calumnies should be punished by the just King in accordance with their offence.

The King should compel the calumniator to pay the sufferer money commensurate with the harm done.

For such persons as steal gems, pearls, gold, and other metals, the punishment should be either the cutting off of the hand or the entire arm, according to the value of the stolen property.

Those who steal buffaloes, horses, cattle, jewels, etc., and infants, should be punished by the King as thieves.

Thieves who steal food and articles of small value should be corrected by being kept on a diet of grains for a week or a fortnight.

O Adored of the Devas! the traitor and the ingrate can never attain liberation by sacrifices, votive observances, penances, acts of charity, and other expiatory rites.

The King should, after severely punishing them, exile from his dominion men who give false evidence, or who are partial as arbitrators.

The testimony of six, four, or even three witnesses is sufficient to prove a fact; but, O Shiva! the testimony of two witnesses of well-known piety is enough.

Beloved! if witnesses contradict one another on questions of place, time, and other details of fact, then their testimony should be rejected.

O Beloved! the word of the blind and the deaf should be accepted as evidence, and the signs and writing of a dumb man and of one who is both deaf and dumb should also be accepted.

Of all evidence and in all cases, and particularly in litigation, documentary evidence is the best, as it does not perish and always endures.

The man who fabricates a writing for his own use or for the use of another should be punished with double the punishment of a false witness.

The statement on oath, on his own behalf, of a careful and unerring man is of a higher probative value than the word of many witnesses.

O Parvvati! as all virtues find their support in Truth, so do all vices find their support in untruth.

Therefore, the King shall incur no blame by chastizing those who are devoid of Truth and are the receptacle of all vices. This is the command of Shiva.

Devi! if a man says, "I tell the truth," at the same time touching any of the following – a Kaula, the Guru, a Brahmana, water of Ganga, an image of a Devata, a Kula religious Book, Kulamrita, or the offerings made to a Deity, he has taken an oath. If after that he speaks an untruth, then he will go to hell for one Kalpa.

An oath that an act which is not sinful will be or will not be done, should always be kept by men.

The man who has broken his oath should purify himself by a fortnight's fast; and one who has broken it by mistake should live on grains for twelve days.

Even the Kula-dharmma, if not followed according to Truth and the injunctions, not only fails to secure final liberation and beatitude, but leads to sin.

Wine is Tara Herself in liquid form, is the Saviour of beings, the Mother of enjoyment and liberation, who destroys danger and diseases, burns up the heaps of sins, and purifies the world.O Beloved! She grants all success, and increases knowledge, intellect, and learning, and, O Adya! She is ever worshipped by those who have attained final liberation and those who are desirous of attaining final liberation, by those that have become and those striving to be adepts, and by Kings and Devas for the attainment of their desires.

Mortals who drink wine with their minds well under control and according to the injunctions (of Shiva) are, as it were, Immortals on earth.

By partaking, in accordance to the injunctions, of any of the tattvas, man becomes like unto Shiva. What, then, is the result of partaking of all the five Tattvas?.

But the drinking of this Devi Varuni in disregard of the injunctions destroys the intellect (understanding), life, fame, and wealth of men.

By the excessive drinking of wine the drunkard destroys the understanding, which is the means for the attainment of the fourfold end of human existence.

Only harm at every step, both to himself and to others, comes out of a man whose mind is distracted and who knows not what should and what should not be done.

Therefore, the King or the Lord of the Chakra should correct by bodily and pecuniary punishments those who are over-addicted to wine and intoxicating drugs.

The understanding of men is clouded by the drinking of wine, whether in small or large quantities, according to the difference in the quality of the wine, to the temperament of the individuals, to the place where and the time when it is taken.

Therefore, excessive drinking is to be judged, not from the quantity drunk, but from the result as shown in difficulty of speech and from the unsteadiness of hands, feet, and sight.

The King should burn the tongues and confiscate the money of, and inflict corporal punishments on, men who hold not their senses under control, whose minds are distracted by drink, who deviate from the duty they owe to Devas and Gurus, who are fearful to behold, who are the source of all folly, who are sinful, and transgressors of the injunctions of Shiva, and bring ruin on themselves.

The King should severely chastise and fine the man who is unsteady in hands, feet, or in speech, who is bewildered, maddened, and beyond himself with drink.

The King, who labours for the happiness of his subjects, should inflict pecuniary punishment on the drunkard who is guilty of evil language and is devoid of fear and shame.

O Kuleshvari! a Kaula, even if he has been initiated a hundred times, should be regarded as a Pashu, and expelled from the Kula community.

The Kaula who drinks excessively of wine, be it consecrated or not, should be renounced by all Kaulas and punished by the King.

The drunken twice-born man who makes his Brahmi wife drink wine should purify both himself and his wife by living on a diet of grains for five days.

The man who has drunk wine which has not been sanctified should purify himself by fasting for three days, and who has eaten meat which has not been sanctified should fast for two days.

If a man partakes of fish and parched food which have not been sanctified, he should fast for a day, but who participates in the fifth tattva without conforming to the rites should be corrected by the King's punishment.

He who knowingly eats human flesh or beef should purify himself by a fortnight's fast. This is the expiation for this sin.

Beloved! a man who has eaten the flesh of animals of human shape, or of carnivorous animals, should purify himself by a three days' fast.

The man who partakes of food cooked by Mlechchhas, Chandalas, and Pashus, who are the enemies of the Kula creed, is purified by a fortnight's fast.

And, O Kuleshvari! if anyone knowingly partakes of the leavings of these, then he should fast for a month to purify himself, and if he has done so unknowingly he should fast for a fortnight.

The injunction is that if a man partakes of food cooked by a man of a caste inferior to his own, he should, to purify himself, fast for three days.

By the partaking of food of a Pashu, Chandala, and Mlechchha, which has been placed in the Chakra or in the hands of a Vira, no sin is incurred.

One who partakes of forbidden food at a time when food is scarce, in times of famine and danger, or when life is at stake, is guiltless of any transgression.

If food is eaten on the back of an elephant, or on a block of stone, or on a piece of wood, which can be carried only by several men, or in places where nothing objectionable is actually perceived, there is no fault.

Animals the flesh of which is forbidden, as also diseased animals, should not be killed even for the purpose of sacrifice to the Devas. By killing such animals sin is incurred.

If anyone knowingly kills a bull, then he shall do penance (as described below), and if he does so unknowingly he shall do half of such penance. This is the command of Shangkara.

So long as the penance is not performed he shall not shave or pare his nails nor wear clean raiments.

Shiva! he should fast for a month, and should live on grains for another month, and should live eating food which he has begged during the third month. This is called Krichchhra-Vrata.

At the end of the penance he should shave his head and free himself from the sin of wilful killing of the bull by feasting Kaulas, relatives (Agnates), and Bandhavas.

If the death of a cow or bull is caused by want of care, the expiation is an eight days' fast for a Brahmana, and for a Kshatriya or inferior castes fasting for six, four, and two days.

O Kaulini! the sin of wilfully slaughtering an elephant or a camel, or a buffalo, or a horse is expiated by a three days' fast.

Expiation for killing a deer, sheep, goat, or a cat, is a fast for one whole day and a night, and one who has killed a peacock, a parrot, or a gander should abstain fom food till sunset of the day on which the sin is committed.

If anyone kills any other inferior animal which possesses bones, he should live on vegetable food for a night. The killing of a boneless animal is expiated by repentance.

There is no blame upon Kings who kill beasts, fish, and oviparous creatures when hunting; for hunting, O Devi! is an immemorial practice among Kings.

Killing should always be avoided, O Gentle One! except if it be for the purpose of sacrifice to a Deva. The man who kills according to the injunctions sins not.

Should a man be unable to complete a religious devotion which he has undertaken, if he walks across the remnants after the worship of any Devata, or if he touches an image of a Deva when he is unclean, then in all such cases he should recite the Gayatri.

The father, the mother, and the giver of the Brahman are the Maha-gurus. He who speaks ill of, or towards, them should, in order to purify himself, fast for five days.

Similarly, O Beloved! if anyone speaks ill of other persons entitled to respect, Kaulas and Vipras, then he should purify himself by fasting two days and a half.

A man may for the acquisition of wealth go to any country, but he should avoid such countries and Shastras as prohibit Kaulika rites.

The man who of his own free-will goes to a country where the Kaula-dharmma is prohibited falls from his status, and should be purified by Purnabhisheka.

In expiatory penance, that which is recognized as a fast is going without food for eight yamas from sunrise.

The fast is, however, not broken should one drink a handful of water or eat the air for the preservation of his life.

If one is unable, by reason of old age or disease, to fast, then, in lieu of each fast, he should feast twelve Brahmanas.

The sins of speaking ill of others, self-laudation, evil habits, impropriety in speech or action, should be expiated by repentance.

All other sins, whether committed knowingly or unknowingly, are destroyed by repeating the Gayatri of the Devi and feeding the Kaulas.

These general rules are applicable to men, women, and the sexless; the only difference is that in the case of the women the husband is their Maha-guru.

Men who are suffering from very great disease and those who are always ailing become purified and entitled to perform rites relating to the Devas and the Pitris by giving away gold.

A house which has been defiled by unnatural death, or which has been struck by lightning, should be purified by one hundred Vyahriti Homas.

If the dead body of an animal possessing bones be found in a lake, tank, or well, then it should be at once taken out, and the same should be purified.

The method of purifying such places is as follows: Twenty-one jars of pure water should, after being consecrated with Purnabhisheka Mantra, be poured into it.

If such places contain but a small quantity of water, and this has been polluted by the stench of the dead body, then they should be dewatered and the loose mud removed therefrom, and when this has been done water should be poured in the manner described.

If they contain water of sufficient quantity to drown an elephant, then a hundred jars of water should be removed, and then consecrated water should be poured into them.

If not so purified, then the waters of the reservoirs polluted by the touch of the dead body become undrinkable, and the reservoir cannot be consecrated.

Bathing in these reservoirs is useless, and any rite performed with their waters becomes fruitless, and any person using the water for any purpose whatever should remain without food for a day and take Panchamrita to purify himself.

Should anyone perchance see a wealthy man who begs, a warrior averse to battle, a detractor of the Kula dharmma, a lady of the family who drinks wine, a man who is a traitor, or a learned man addicted to sin, then in any of these cases he should view the Sun, utter the name of Vishnu, and bathe in the clothes which he is wearing at the time.

Men of the twice-born classes should, if they sell donkeys, fowls, or swine, or if they engage in any low pursuits, purify themselves by observing the three days' vrata.

The Tri-dina-vrata, O Ambika! is thus performed: the first day is to be spent in fasting, the second day is to be spent in eating grain meals only, and the third in drinking water only.

The man who, without being asked, enters a room the door of which is closed, and one who speaks of things which he has been asked to keep secret, should go without food for five days.

The man who from pride fails to rise when he sees anyone worthy of veneration coming towards him, or when he sees the Kula Scriptures being brought in, should go without food for a day in order to purify himself.

In this Shastra spoken by Shiva the meanings of the words used are plain; those who put far-fetched meanings upon them go the downward path.

I have spoken to thee, O Devi! of that which is the Essence of essences, of that which is above the most excellent, of that which conduces to the well-being (of men) in this world and the next, as also of that which is both purifying and beneficent and according to Dharmma.

End of the Eleventh Joyful Message, entitled "The Account of Expiatory Rites."

Chapter 12

An Account of the Eternal and Immutable Dharmma

SHRI SADASHIVA said:

O Primordial One! I am speaking to Thee again of the everlasting laws; the wise King may easily rule his subjects if he follows them.

If Kings did not establish rules, men in their covetousness would quarrel among themselves, even with their friends, relatives, and their superiors.

These self-seeking men, O Devi! would for the sake of wealth kill one another, and be full of sin by reason of their maliciousness and desire to thieve.

It is therefore for their good that I am laying down the rule in accordance with Dharmma, by following which men will not swerve from the right (path).

As the King should punish the wicked for the removal of their sins, so should he also divide the inheritance according to the relationship.

Relationship is of two kinds–by marriage and by birth; of these, relationship by birth is stronger than relationship by marriage.

In inheritance, O Shiva! descendants have a stronger claim than ascendants, and in this order of descendants and ascendants the males are better qualified for inheritance than females.

But among these, again, the proximate relation is entitled to the inheritance; the wise ones should divide the property according to this rule and in this order:

If the deceased leaves son, grandson, daughters, father, wife, and other relations, then the son is entitled to the whole of the inheritance, and not the others.

If there are several sons, they are all entitled to equal shares. (In the case of a King) the kingdom goes to the eldest son, but that is in accordance to the custom of the family.

If there be any paternal debt which should be paid out of the paternal property, such property should not be divided.

If men should divide and take paternal property, then the King should take it from them, and discharge the paternal debt.

As men go to hell by reason of their own sins, so they are bound by their individually incurred debts, and others are not.

Whatever general property there may be, either immovable or of other kinds, sharers shall get the same according to their respective shares.

The division is complete on the co-partners agreeing to it. If they do not agree, then the King should divide it impartially.

The King should divide the value or profits of property which is incapable of division, whether the same be immovable or movable.

If a man proves his right to a share after the property is divided, then the King should divide the property over again, and give the person entitled his share.

O Shiva! the King should punish the man who, after property is once divided by the consent of the co-partners, quarrels again with respect to it.

If the deceased dies leaving behind him grandson, wife, and father, then the grandson is entitled to the property by reason of his being a descendant.

If the childless man leaves (surviving him) father, brother, and grandfather, then the father inherits the property by reason of the closeness of consanguinity.

Beloved! if the deceased leaves daughters (surviving him), although they are closer to him, yet the grandsons (sons' sons) are entitled to his property, because man is prior.

From the grandfather the property goes to the grandson by the deceased son, and thus it is that men proclaim that the father's self is in the image of the son.

In marital relationship the Brahmi wife is the superior, and the sonless man's property should go to the wife, who is half his body.

The sonless widow, however, is not competent to sell or give away property inherited from her husband, except what is her own by her own right.

Anything given by the fathers and fathers-in-law approved by Dharmma, whatever is earned by her personal efforts, is to be recognized as "Woman's property".

On her death it goes to the husband, and to his heirs according to the grades of descendants and ancestors.

If the woman remains faithful to her Dharmma, and lives under the control of the relations of her husband, and in their absence under the control of her father's relations, then only is she entitled to inherit.

The woman who is even likely to go astray is not entitled to inherit the husband's property. She is merely entitled to a living allowance from the heirs of her husband.

If the man who has died has many wives, all of whom are pious, then, O Thou of pure Smiles! they are entitled to the husband's property in equal shares.

If the woman who inherits her husband's property dies leaving daughters, then the property is taken to have gone back from the husband and from him to the daughter.

In this way, if there is a daughter and the property goes to the son's widow, then, on the death of the latter, it would go back to the husband, and from the father-in-law descend to the daughter of the latter.

Similarly, O Shiva! if property goes to the mother in the lifetime of the paternal grandfather, then, on her death, it goes to her father-in-law through her son and husband.

As the property of the deceased ascends to the father, so it also ascends to the mother if she is a widow.

But the stepmother shall not inherit if the mother is living, but on the death of the mother it goes to the stepmother through the father.

Where, in the absence of descendants, the inheritance cannot descend, it would ascend the same way by which it would descend.

Therefore, even when the father's brother is alive, the daughter inherits the property, and if she dies childless then such property goes to the father's brother.

As inheritance descends in the male line, the stepbrother inherits even when there is a uterine sister.

And when there is a uterine sister and sons of stepbrother, it is the latter who inherit the property.

If the deceased leaves (surviving him) both uterine and stepbrother, then, by reason of the property descending through the father, they are entitled to inherit in equal shares.

In the lifetime of their daughters their sons are not entitled to inherit until the obstruction is removed by the death of the daughters.

In the absence of sons, the daughters divide among themselves the paternal property, after deducting the marriage expenses of an unmarried daughter (if any) out of the general estate.

On the death of a childless woman the stri-dhana goes to her husband, and the property which she inherited from anyone else goes back to the line of the person from whom she inherited.

The woman may spend property inherited by her on her own maintenance, and she may spend profits of it on acts of religious merit, but she is not able to sell or make gifts of it.

Where the daughter-in-law of the grandfather (father's father) is living, or the stepmother of the father is living, the inheritance goes to the grandfather, and through his son to the (grandfather's) daughter-in-law.

Where the grandfather, the father's brother, and the brother are living, the brother succeeds by reason of the priority in claim of the descendant.

If a man dies leaving him surviving his grandfather, brother, and uncle, both of the former are nearer in degree – than the last, and the property descends through the father to the deceased's brother.

If the deceased leaves a daughter's son and father (surviving him), then the daughter's son inherits, because property in the first place descends.

If both the father and the mother of the deceased be living (at his death), then, O Kalika! by reason of the superior claim of the male, the father takes his property.

If the mother's brother is living, the sapindas of the father take the property of the deceased by reason of the superior claim of the paternal relationship.

Property failing to go downwards has (here) gone upwards, but, O Shiva! by reason of the superior claim of the male line it has gone to the father's family. The mother's brother, in spite of the nearness of his relationship, does not inherit.

The grandson by a deceased son inherits from his grandfather's estate the share which his father would have inherited along with his (the father's) brothers.

Similarly, the granddaughter who has no brother and whose parents are dead, inherits, if she be well conducted, her grandfather's (father's father) property with her father's brothers.

On the death of the grandfather leaving him surviving his wife, his daughter, and granddaughter, the last, O Devi! is the heiress of the property, since she takes it through her father.

In property which descends the male among the descendants, and in property which ascends, the male among the ascendants, are pre-eminently qualified (to inherit).

Therefore, O Beloved! if the deceased has daughter-in-law, granddaughter, and daughter surviving him, then his father cannot take the property.

If there is no one in the family of the father of the deceased entitled to inherit his property, then in manner above indicated it goes to the family of his mother's father.

Property which has gone to the maternal grandfather shall ascend and descend, and go both to males and females through the maternal uncle and his sons and others.

If the line of Brahmi marriage, or if the sapindas of the father or of the mother, be in existence, then the issue of the Shaiva marriage are not entitled to inherit the father's property.

The wife and children of the Shaiva marriage, O Gentle One! are entitled to receive, from the person who inherits the property of the deceased, their food and clothes in proportion to the property left.Beloved! the Shaiva wife, if well conducted, is entitled to be maintained by the Shaiva husband alone. She has no claim to the property of her father and others.

Therefore, the father who marries his well-born daughter according to Shaiva rites by reason of anger or covetousness will be despised of men.

In the absence of issue of the Shaiva marriage, the Sodaka, the Guru, and the King shall, by the injunctions of Shiva, take the property of the deceased.

Beloved! men within the seventh degree are sapindas, and beyond them to the seventh degree are sodakas, and beyond them are Gotra-jas merely.

Where property which has been divided is again wilfully mixed together, it should be divided again as if it had not been divided.

The heirs of a deceased are on his death entitled to such share of property, whether partitioned or not partitioned, as the deceased himself was entitled to.

Those who inherit the property of another should offer him pindas as long as they live; it is otherwise in the case–of a son by Shaiva marriage.

Just as the rules relating to uncleanliness should, in this world, be observed by reason of birth-connection, so they should be observed for three nights by reason of connection by heirship.

The twice-born and other classes shall purify themselves by observing the rules as to uncleanliness from the day they hear the cause of it until the end of the period prescribed; this is so both in the case of Purnashaucha and of Khandashaucha.

If the period has expired when one hears the cause of it, then there is no Khandashaucha. And as regards Purnashaucha, it should be observed for only three days, but if one hears of the cause of the uncleanliness after the lapse of a year there is no period of uncleanliness to be observed.

If a son hears of his father's or mother's death, or if the faithful wife hears of her husband's death after one year, then the son or the widow shall observe the period of uncleanliness for three nights.

If during the continuance of a period of uncleanliness another new period begins, then the period comes to an end with the end of the Garu-ashaucha.

The degree of different kinds of uncleanliness depends on the greater or lesser length of the period which should be observed. Of the various kinds of uncleanliness, that which is extensive in point of time is greater than that which is less extensive.

If on the last day of a period of uncleanliness another period commences, then the uncleanliness is removed on the last day of the first period of uncleanliness; but if the cause of uncleanliness be such as to necessitate the observance of the full period, then the pre-existing period should be extended by two days.

The unmarried female shall observe the period of uncleanliness of the father's family, but after she is married she is to observe impurity for three days on the death of her parents.

After her marriage the wife becomes of the same gotra as her husband; the adopted son similarly becomes of the same gotra as the person who adopts him.

A son should be adopted with consent of his father and mother, and at the time of adoption the adopted should, with his kinsmen, perform the sacramental rites, mentioning his own gotra and name.

The adopted son shall have the same right to the property of his adoptive mother and father, and the same rights to offer pindas to them as the natural-born son has, since they are his mother and father.

A boy of less than five years of age and of one's own caste should be adopted and brought up; a boy of over five years of age is not eligible.

O Kalika! if a brother adopts his brother's son, then the brother adopting becomes the father, and the natural father becomes the uncle of the boy so adopted.

He who inherits the property of another should observe the Dharmma of the person he inherits; he should also follow his family custom and please his kinsmen.

In the case of the death of kaninas, golakas, kundas, and persons guilty of great sins, there is no uncleanliness to be observed, and they are not qualified to inherit.

In the case of the death of a man who has been punished by castration, or of a woman who has been punished by the cutting of her nose, or of persons guilty of very great sins, there is no period of uncleanliness to be observed.

The King should for twelve years protect the family and property of those of whom no news is known, and who have disappeared without any trace of their whereabouts.

On the expiration of twelve years the image of such a person should be made with kusha grass and cremated. His children and others should observe a period of uncleanliness for three days, and liberate him from the condition of a Preta.

The King should then divide his property among the members of his family in their order, beginning with the son; otherwise he (the King) incurs sin.

The King should protect the man who has no protector, who is powerless, who is in the midst of adversity, because the King is the Lord of his subjects.

Kalika! if the man who has disappeared returns after the lapse of twelve years, then he shall recover his wife, children, and property; there is no doubt of that.

Even a man is not competent to give away ancestral, immovable property, either to his own people or to strangers, without the consent of his heirs.

A man may, at his pleasure, give away self-acquired property, be it movable or immovable, and may also give away ancestral movable property.

If there be a son or wife living, or daughter or daughter's son, or father or mother, or brother or sister, even then one may give away self-acquired property, both movable and immovable, and inherited movable property.

If a man gives away or dedicates such property to any religious object, then his sons and others cannot affect such gift or dedication.

Property dedicated to any religious object should be looked after by the giver. The latter is, however, not competent to take it back, because the ownership of such property is Dharmma.

Ambika! the property or the profits thereof should be employed by the dedicator himself, or his agent, for the religious object to which it was dedicated.

If the proprietor out of affection gives away half his self-acquired property to anyone, then his heirs shall not be able to annul the gift.

If the proprietor gives half his self-acquired wealth to any of his heirs, in such a case the other heirs shall not be able to avoid such gift.

If one of several brothers earns money with the help of the paternal property, then, while the other brothers are entitled to proportionate shares of the paternal property, no one but the acquirer is entitled to the profits.

If one brother acquires ancestral property which was lost, then he shall receive two shares, and the other brothers shall together receive one share.

Religious merit, wealth, and learning are all dependent on the body, and inasmuch as this body comes from the father, then (in such sense) what is there which is not paternal property?.

If whatever men earn, even when separate in mess and separate in property, is to be considered paternal property, then what is there that is self-acquired?.

Therefore, O Great Devi! whatever money is earned by one's own individual labour shall be self-acquired; the person acquiring it shall be the owner thereof, and no one else.

O Devi! the man who even lifts his hand against his mother, father, Guru, paternal and maternal grandfathers, shall not inherit.

The man who kills another shall not inherit his property; but the other heirs of the person killed shall inherit his property.

Ambika! eunuchs and persons who are crippled are entitled to food and clothes so long as they live, but they are not entitled to inherit property.

If a man finds property which belongs to another, on the road or anywhere else, then the King shall, after due deliberation, make the finder restore it to the owner.

If a man finds property, or a beast of which there is no owner, then the finder becomes the owner of the same, but should give the King a tenth share of such property or beast (or of the value thereof).

If there be a competent buyer for immovable property, who is a near relation, then it is not competent for the owner of the immovable property to sell the same to another.

Among buyers who are near, the agnate and one of the same caste are specially qualified, and in their absence friends, but the desire of the seller should prevail.

If immovable property is about to be sold at a price fixed, and a neighbour pays the same price, then the latter is entitled to purchase it and no other.

If the neighbour is unable to pay the price and consents to the sale (to another), then only may the householder sell the property to another.

O Devi! if immovable property be bought without the knowledge of the neighbour, the latter is entitled to have it upon the condition of his paying the price immediately he hears of such sale.

Should, however, the buyer, after purchasing it, have converted the place into a garden, or built a house thereon, or if he has pulled down any building, the neighbour is not entitled in such a case to obtain the immovable property by the payment of its price.

A man may, without permission, without payment, and without obstruction, bring under cultivation any land which rises from the water, which is in the middle of a forest, or otherwise difficult of access.

Where land has been brought under cultivation by considerable labour, the King, since he is the Lord of the soil, should be given a tenth of the profits of the land, and the rest should be enjoyed by him who has reclaimed it.

One should not excavate tanks, reservoirs, or wells, nor plant trees, nor build houses in places where they are likely to injure other people.

All have the right to drink the water of tanks and wells dedicated to Devas, as also the water of rivers, but the neighbours alone have the right to bale it out.

The water should not be baled out of tanks, etc., even by neighbours, if to do so would cause a water famine.

The mortgage and sale of property which is undivided without the consent of the co-sharers, as also when the right of the parties therein is not determined, is invalid.

If property mortgaged or deposited with another is destroyed wilfully or by negligence, then the King should make the mortgagee or depositee restore the value thereof to the owner.

If any animal or any other thing is used with the consent of the depositor by the person with whom they are placed, then the depositee should bear the expense of food and keep.

Where immovable or movable property is made over to another for profit, such transaction will be invalid if it be not for a definite time, or if the amount of profits is indeterminate.

Common (joint) property should not, on the father's death, be employed for profit without the consent of all the co-sharers.

If articles are sold at improper prices, then the King may set aside such sale.

As a body is born and dies only once, and property can be given away only once, so there can be but one Brahma marriage of the daughter.

The man, devoted to his ancestors, who has an only son, should not give him away (in adoption), and, similarly, he should not give away an only wife or an only daughter in Shaiva marriage.

In rites relating to the Devas and the Pitris, in mercantile transactions, and in Courts of law, whatever the substitute (Agent) does is the act of the employer.

The immutable rule is that the Agent or emissary should not be punished for the guilt of the employer.

In monetary dealings, in agriculture, in mercantile transactions, as also in all other dealings, whatever is undertaken, the same should be performed if in agreement with Dharmma.

The Lord protects this universe. Whoever wish to destroy it will be themselves destroyed, and whosoever protect it them the Lord of the Universe Himself protects. Therefore should one act for the good of the world.

End of Twelfth Joyful Message, entitled, "An Account of the Eternal and Immutable Dharmma."

Chapter 13

Installation of the Devata

PARVATI, the Mother of the three worlds, Her mind engrossed with thoughts for the purification of men polluted with the impurities of the Kali Age, humbly asked Mahesha, the Deva among Devas, who had thus spoken of the essence of all the Nigamas, which is the seed of heaven and final liberation (as follows):

Shri Devi said:

How should the form of Mahakali be thought of, She who is the Great Cause, the Primordial Energy, the Great Effulgence, more subtle than the subtlest elements?.

It is only that which is the work of Prakriti which has form. How should She have form? She is above the most high. It behoves thee, O Deva! to completely remove this doubt of mine.

Shri Sadashiva said:

Beloved! I have already said that to meet the needsof the worshippers the image of the Devi is formed according to Her qualities and actions.

As white, yellow, and other colours all disappear in black, in the same way, O Shailaja! all beings enter Kali.

Therefore it is that by those who have attained the knowledge of the means of final liberation, the attributeless, formless, and beneficent Kalashakti is endowed with the colour of blackness.

As the eternal and inexhaustible One image of Kala and soul of beneficence is nectar itself, therefore the sign of the Moon is placed on her forehead. As She surveys the entire universe, which is the product of time, with Her three eyes – the Moon, the Sun, and Fire – therefore she is endowed with three eyes.

As She devours all existence, as She chews all things existing with her fierce teeth, therefore a mass of blood is imagined to be the apparel of the Queen of the Devas (at the final dissolution).

As time after time She protects all beings from danger, and as She directs them in the paths of duty, her hands are lifted up to dispel fear and grant blessings.

As She encompasses the universe, which is the product of Rajoguna, she is spoken of, O Gentle One! as the Devi who is seated on the red lotus, gazing at Kala drunk with intoxicating wine and playing with the universe. The Devi also, whose substance is intelligence, witnesseth all things.

It is for the benefit of such worshippers as are of weak intelligence that the different shapes are formed according to the attributes (of the Divinity).

Shri Devi said:

What merit does the worshipper gain who makes an image of the Great Devi of mud, stone, wood, or metal, in accordance with the representation described by Thee for the salvation of humanity, and who decks the same with clothes and jewels, and who, in a beautifully decorated house, consecrates it?.

O Lord! out of Thy kindness for me, reveal this also, with all the particular rules according to which the image of the Devi should be consecrated.

Thou hast already spoken of the consecration of Tanks, Wells, Houses, Gardens, and the images of Devas, but Thou didst not speak in detail.

I wish to hear the injunctions relating to them from thy lotus-mouth. Out of thy kindness, speak, O Para-meshana! if it pleases Thee.

Shri Sadashiva said:

O Parameshvari! this supreme essence about which Thou hast asked is very mysterious. Do thou, therefore, listen attentively.

There are two classes of men – those who act with, and without, a view to the fruits of action. The latter attain final liberation. I am now speaking of the former.

Beloved! the man who consecrates the image of a Deva goes to the region of such Deva, and enjoys that which is there attainable.

He who consecrates an image of mud stays in such region for ten thousand kalpas. He who consecrates an image of wood stays there ten times that period. In the case of the consecration of a stone image the length of stay is ten times the latter period, and in the case of the consecration of a metal image it is ten times the last-mentioned period.

Listen to the merit which is acquired by the man who, in the name of any Deva, or for the attainment of any desire, builds and consecrates and gives away a temple made of timber and thatch and other materials, or renovates such a temple, decorated with flags and images of the carriers of the Deva.

He who gives away a thatched temple shall live in the region of the Devas for one thousand koti years.

He who gives away a brick-built temple shall live a hundred times that period, and he who gives away a stone-built temple, ten thousand times the last-mentioned period.

Adya! the man who builds a bridge or causeway shall not see the region of Yama, but will happily reach the abode of the Suras, and will there have enjoyment in their company.

He who dedicates trees and gardens goes to the region of the Devas, and lives in celestial houses surrounded by Kalpa trees in the enjoyment of all desired and agreeable enjoyments.

Those who give away ponds and the like for the comfort of all beings are washed of all sins, and, having attained the blissful region of Brahma, reside there a hundred years for each drop of water which they contain.

Devi! the man who dedicates the image of a Vahana for the pleasure of any Deva shall live continually in the region of such Deva, protected by Him.

Ten times the merit which is acquired on earth by the gift of a Vahana made of mud is acquired by the gift of one made of wood, and ten times the latter is acquired by the gift of one made of stone. Should one made of brass or bell-metal or copper, or any other metal, be given, then the merit is multiplied in each case tenfold.

The excellent worshipper should present a great lion to the temple of Devi, a bull to the temple of Shangkara, and a Garuda to the temple of Keshava.

The geat lion has sharp teeth, a ferocious mouth, and mane on his neck and shoulder. The claws of his four feet are as hard as the thunderbolt.

The bull is armed with horns, is white of body, and has four black hoofs, a large hump, black hair at the end of his tail, and a black shoulder.

The Garuda is winged, has thighs like a bird, and a face like a man's, with a long nose. He is seated on his haunches, with folded palms.

By the present of flags and flag-staffs the Devas remain pleased for a hundred years. The flag-staff should be thirty-two cubits long, and should be strong, without defects, straight, and pleasant to look at. It should be wrapped round with a red cloth, with a chakra at its top

The flag should be attached to the top of the staff, and should be marked with the image of the carrier of the particular Devata. It should be broad at the part nearest the staff and narrow at the other end. It should be made of fine cloth. In short, whatever ornaments the top of the flag-staff is a flag.

Whatever a man presents with faith and devotion in the name of a Deva, be it clothes, jewels, beds, carriages, vessels for drinking and eating, pan plates, spittoon, precious stones, pearl, coral, gems, or anything else with which he is pleased, such a man will reach the region of such Deva and receive in turn a Koti times the presents he made.

Those who worship with the object of attaining a particular reward gain such reward which (however) is as destructible as a kingdom acquired in a dream. Those, however, who rightly act without hope of reward attain nirvana, and are released from rebirth.

In ceremonies relating to the dedication of a reservoir of water, a house, a garden, a bridge, a causeway, a Devati, or a tree, the Vastu Spirit should be carefully worshipped.

The man who performs any of these ceremonies without worshipping the Vastu-Daitya is troubled by the Vastu-Daitya and his followers.

The twelve followers of the Vastu Daitya are Kapi-lasya, Pingakesha, Bhishana, Raktalochana, Kotara-raksha, Lambakarna, Dirghajanggha, Mahodara, Ashvatunda, Kakakantha, Vajravahu, and Vratantaka, and these followers of Vastu should be propitiated with great care.

Now, listen! I am speaking of the Mandala where the Vastu-Purusha should be worshipped.

On an altar or on a level space, which has been well washed with pure water, a straight line should be drawn, one cubit in length, from the Vayu to the Ishana corner.

In the same manner another line should be drawn from the Ishana to the Agni corner, and another from the Agni to the Nairita corner, and then from the Nairita to the Vayu corner.

By these straight lines a square mandala should be drawn. Then two lines should be drawn from corner to corner (diagonally) to divide the mandala into four parts, like four fish-tails.

The wise man should then draw two lines, one from the West to the East, and the other from the North to the South, through the point where the diagonal lines cut one another, so as to pass through the tip of the fish-tails.

Then four diagonal lines should be drawn connecting the corners of the four inner squares so formed by the lines at each of the corners.

According to these rules, sixteen rooms should be drawn with five different colours, and an excellent yantra thus made.

In the four middle rooms draw a beautiful lotus with four petals, the pericarp of yellow and red colour, and the filaments of red.

The petals may be white or yellow, and the interstices may be coloured with any colour chosen.

Beginning with the corner of Shambhu, the twelve rooms should be filled up with the four colours – viz., white, black, yellow, and red.

In filling up the rooms one should go towards one's right, and in the worship of the Devas therein one should go to the left.

The Vastu Spirit should be worshipped in the lotus, and the twelve daityas, Kapilasya and others, should be worshipped in the twelve rooms, beginning with the Ishana corner.

Fire should be consecrated according to the injunctions laid down for Kushandika, and after offer of oblations to the best of one's ability, the Vastu-yajna should be concluded.

I have thus described, O Devi! the auspicious Vastu worship, by the performance of which a man never suffers dangers from Vastu (and his followers).

Shri Devi said:

Thou hast described the mandala of, and the injunctions relating to, the worship of Vastu, but thou hast not spoken of the Dhyana, my husband; do thou now reveal it.

Shri Sadashiva said:

I am speaking of Dhyana of the Vastu-Rakshasa, by constant and devoted repetition of which all dangers are destroyed. O Maheshani! do thou listen.

The Deva Vastu-pati should be meditated upon as four-armed, of great body, his head covered with matted hair, three eyed, of ferocious aspect, decked with garlands and earrings, with big belly and long ears and hairy body, wearing yellow garments, holding in his hand the mace, the trident, the axe, and the Khatvanga. Let him be pictured as (red) like the rising Sun and like the God of Death to one's enemies, seated in the padmasana posture on the back of a tortoise, surrounded by Kapilasya and other powerful followers, carrying swords and shields.

Whenever there is panic caused by pestilence or epidemics, an apprehension of any public calamity, danger to one's children, or fear arising from ferocious beasts or Rakshasas, then Vastu with his followers should be meditated upon as above, and then worshipped, and thus all manner of peace may be obtained by the offer of oblations of sesamum-seeds, ghee, and payasa.

O Suvrata! in these rites the Grahas and the ten Dikpalas should be worshipped in the same way as Vastu is worshipped.

Brahma, Vishnu, Rudra, Vani, Lakshmi, the celestial mothers, Ganesha, and the Vasus, should also be worshipped.

O Kalika! if in these rites the Pitris are not satisfied, then all which is done becomes fruitless, and there is danger in every stage.

Therefore, O Maheshi! in all these rites Abhyudayika. Shraddha should be performed for the satisfaction of the Pitris.

I shall now speak of the Graha-yantra, which is the cause of all kinds of peace. If Indra and all the planets are worshipped, then they grant every desire.

In order to draw the yantra three triangles should be drawn with a circle outside them, and outside, but touching the circle, eight petals should be drawn.

Then should a beautiful Bhupura be drawn (outside the yantra) with four entrances, and (outside the Bhupura) between the East and North-East corners a circle should be drawn with its diameter the length of a pradesha, and between the West and the South-West corners another similar circle should be drawn.

Then the nine corners should be filled up with colours of the nine planets, and the left and right sides of the two inner triangles should be

155

made white and yellow, and the base should be black. The eight petals should be filled up with the colours of the eight regents of the quarters.

The walls of the Bhupura should be decorated with white, red, and black powders, and, O Devi! the two circles outside the Bhupura should be coloured red and white, and the intervening spaces of the yantra may be coloured in any manner the wise may choose.

Listen now to the order in which each planet should be worshipped in the particular chambers, and in which each Dikpati should be worshipped in the particular petals, and as to the names of the Devas who are present at each particular entrance.

In the inner triangle the Sun should be worshipped, and in the angles of the two sides Aruna and Shikha. Behind him with the garland of rays the two standards of the two fierce ones (Shikha and Aruna) should be worshipped.

Worship the maker of nights in the corner above the Sun on the East, in the Agni corner Mangala, on the South side Budha, in the Nairrita corner Vrihaspati, on the West Shukra, in the Vayu corner Shani, in the corner on the North Rahu, and in the Ishana corner Ketu, and, lastly, round about the Moon the multitude of stars. Sun is red, Moon is white, Mangala is tawny, Budha is pale or yellowish-white, Vrihaspati is yellow, Shukra is white, Shani is black, and Rahu and Ketu are of variegated colour; thus I have spoken of the different colours of the Grahas.

The Sun should be meditated upon as having four hands, in two of which he is holding lotuses; and of the other two, one hand is lifted up to dispel fear, and the other makes the sign of blessing. The Moon should be meditated upon as having nectar in one hand, and the other hand in the attitude of giving. Mangala should be meditated upon as slightly bent and holding a staff in his hands. Budha, the son of Moon, should be meditated upon as a boy, the locks of whose hair play about upon his forehead. Guru should be meditated upon with a sacred thread, and holding a book in one hand and a string of Rudraksha beads in the other; and the Guru of Daityas should be meditated upon as blind of one eye, and Shani as lame, and Rahu as a trunkless head, and Ketu as a headless trunk, both deformed and wicked.

Having worshipped each of the planets in this manner, the eight Dikpalas, Indra and others, beginning from the East, should be worshipped.

He of a thousand eyes, of a yellow colour, should first be worshipped. He is dressed in yellow silk garments, and, holding the thunder in his hand, is seated on Airavata.

The body of Agni is of red hue. He is seated on a goat; in his hand is the Shakti. Yama is black, and, holding a staff in his hand, is seated on

156

a bison. Nirriti is of dark green colour, and, holding a sword in his hand, is seated on a horse. Varuna is white, and, seated on an alligator, holds a noose in his hand. Vayu should be meditated on as possessed of a black radiance, seated on a deer and holding a hook. Kuvera is of the colour of gold, and seated on a jewelled lion-seat, holding the noose and hook in his hands. He is surrounded by Yakshas, who are singing his praises. Ishana is seated on the bull; he holds the trident in one hand, and with the other bestows blessings, He is dressed in raiments of tiger-skin, and his effulgence is like that of the full moon.

Having thus meditated upon and worshipped them in their order, Brahma should be worshipped in the upper circle, which is outside the mandala, and Vishnu in the lower one. Then the Devatas at the entrances should be worshipped.

Ugra, Bhima, Prachanda, and Isha, are at the eastern entrance; Jayanta, Kshetra-pala, Nakulesha, and Vrihat-shirah, are at the southern entrance; at the door on the west are Vrika, Ashva, Ananda, and Durjaya; and Trishirah, Purajit, Bhimanada, and Mahodara are at the northern entrance. As protectors of the entrances, they are all armed with weapons, offensive and defensive.

Suvrata! listen to the meditation on Brahma and Ananta. Brahma is of the colour of the red lotus, and has four hands and four faces. He is seated on a swan. With two of his hands he makes the signs which dispel fear and grant boons, and in the others he holds a garland and a book. Ananta is white as the snow, the Kunda flower, or the Moon. He has a thousand hands and a thousand faces, and he should be meditated upon by Suras and Asuras (99-101).

Beloved! I have now spoken of the meditation, the mode of worship, and the yantra. Now, my beloved, listen to their Mantras in their order, beginning with the Vastu Mantra.

Mantras

When Ksha-kara is placed on the Carrier of Oblations. and the long vowels are then added to it, and ornamented with the nada-vindu, the six-lettered Vastu Mantra is formed.

The Suryya Mantra is thus formed: first the tara should be said; then the Maya; then the word tigma-rashme; then the word arogya-daya (in the dative singular); and, last of all, the wife of Fire.

The recognized or approved Mantra of Soma is formed by saying the vijas of Kama, Maya and Vani, then Amrita-kara, amritam plavaya plavaya svaha.

The Mantra of Mangala is proclaimed to be Aing hrang hring sarva-dushtan nashaya nashaya svaha.

The Mantra of the son of Soma is Hrang, Shring, Saumya sarvan kaman puraya svaha(107).

The Mantra of the Sura-Guru is formed thus: Let the tara precede and follow the Vija of Vani, and then say, Abhishtam yachchha yachchha, and lastly svaha.

The Mantra of Shukra is Shang, Shing, Shung, Shaing, Shaung, Shngah.

The Mantra of the Slowly Moving One is Hrang hrang hring hring sarva-shatrun vidravaya vidravaya Martan-dasunave namah – Destroy, destroy all enemies – I bow to the son of Martanda.

The Mantra of Rahu is Rang, Hraung, Bhraung, Hring – Soma-shatro shatrun vidhvangsaya vidhvangsaya Rahave namah--O Enemy of Soma (Moon)! destroy, destroy all enemies. I bow to Rahu.

Krung, Hrung, Kraing to Ketu – is proclaimed to be the Mantra of Ketu.

Lang, Rang, Mring, Strung, Vang, Yang, Kshang, Haung, Vring, and Ang are in their order the ten Mantras of the ten Dikpalas, beginning with Indra and ending with Ananta.

The names of the other attendant Devas are their Mantras; in all instances where there is no Mantra mentioned this is the rule..

Sovereign Mistress of the Devas! the wise man should not add Namah to Mantras that end with the word Namah, nor should he put the wife of Vahni to a Mantra that ends with Svaha.

To the Planets and others should be given flowers, clothes, and jewels, but the colour of the gifts should be the same as that of the respective Planets; otherwise they are not pleased.

The wise man should place fire in the manner prescribed for Kushandika, and perform homa either with flowers of variegated colours or with sacred fuel.

In rites for the attainment of peace or good fortune, or nourishment or prosperity, the Carrier of Oblations is called Varada; in rites relating to consecration he is called Lohitaksha; in destructive rites he is called Shatruha.

Maheshani! in Shanti, Pushti, and Krura rites the man who sacrifices to the Planets will obtain the desired end.

As in the rites relating to the consecration the Devas should be worshipped and libations offered to the Pitris, so also should there be the same sacrifices to Vastu and the Planets.

Should one have to perform two or three consecratory and sacrificial rites on the same day, then the worship of the Devas, the Shraddha of the Pitris, and consecration of fire are required once only.

One who desires the fruit of his observances should not give to any Deva reservoirs of water, houses, gardens, bridges, causeways, carriers, conveyances, clothes, jewels, drinking-cups, and eating-plates, or whatever else he may desire to give, without first sanctifying the same.

In all rites performed with an ultimate object the wise one should in all cases perform a sangkalpa, in accordance with directions, for the full attainment of the good object.

Complete merit is earned when the thing about to be given is first sanctified, worshipped, and mentioned by name, and then the name of him to whom it is given is pronounced.

I will now tell you the Mantras for the consecration of reservoirs of water, houses, gardens, bridges, and cause-ways. The Mantras should always be preceded by the Brahma-Vidya.

Mantras

Reservoir of Water! thou that givest life to all beings! thou that art presided over by Varuna! may this consecration of thee (by me) give satisfaction to all beings that live and move in water, on land, and in air.

House made of timber and grass! thou art the favourite of Brahma; I am consecrating thee with water; do thou be always the cause of pleasure.

When consecrating a house made of bricks and other materials, one should say: "House made of bricks," etc..

Mantras

Garden! thou art pleasant by reason of thy fruits, leaves, and branches, and by thy shadows. I am sprinkling thee with the sacred water (of sacred places); grant me all my wishes.

Bridge! thou art like the bridge across the Ocean of Existence, thou art welcome to the wayfarer; do thou, being consecrated by me, grant me the fitting reward thereof.

Causeway! I am consecrating thee, as thou helpest people in going from one place to another: do thou likewise help me in my way to Heaven.

The wise ones shall use the same Mantra in consecrating a tree as is prescribed for the sprinkling of a garden.

In consecrating all other things, the Pranava, Varuna, and Astra should be used.

Those vahanas that can (or ought to be) bathed should be bathed with the Brahma-gayatri; others should be purified by arghya-water taken up with the ends of kusha grass.

After performing prana-pratishtha, calling it by its name, the vahana called by its name should be duly worshipped, and when decked out should be given to the Devata.

Whilst consecrating a reservoir, Varuna, the lord of aquatic animals, should be worshipped. In the case of a house, Brahma, the lord of all things born, should there be worshipped. Whilst consecrating a garden, a bridge a causeway, Vishnu, who is the protector of the universe, the soul of all, who witnesseth all and is omnipresent, should be worshipped.

Shri Devi said:

Thou hast spoken of the different injunctions relating to the different rites, but thou hast not yet shown the order in which man should practise them.

Rites not properly performed according to the order enjoined do not, even though performed with labour, yield the full benefit to men who follow the life of Karmma.

Shri Sadashiva said:

O Parameshani! thou art beneficent like a mother. What thou hast said is indeed the best for men whose minds are occupied with the results (of their efforts).

The practices relating to the aforementioned rites are different. Devi! I am relating them in their order, beginning with the Vastu-yaga. Do thou listen attentively.

(He who wishes to perform the Vastu-yaga) should the day previous thereto live on a regulated or a restricted diet. After bathing in the early auspicious hour of morning, and performing the ordinary daily religious duties, he should worship the Guru and Narayana.

The worshipper should then, after making sangkalpa, worship Ganesha and others for the attainment of his own object, according to the rules shown in the ordinances.

Dhyana

Worship Ganapati who is of the colour of the Bandhuka flower, and has three eyes; whose head is that of the best of elephants; whose sacred thread is made of the King of Snakes; who is holding in his four lotus hands the conch, the discus, the sword, and a spotless lotus; on whose forehead is the rising young moon; the shining effulgence of whose body and raiments is like that of the Sun; who is decked with various jewels, and is seated on a red lotus.

Having thus meditated upon and worshipped Ganesha to the best of his ability, he should worship Brahma, Vani, Vishnu, and Lakshmi.

Then, after worshipping Shiva, Durga, the Grahas, the sixteen mothers, and the Vasus in the Vasudhara, he should perform the Vriddhishraddha.

Then the mandala of the Vastu-daitya should be drawn, and there the Vastu-daitya with his followers should be worshipped.

Then there make a sthandila and purifying fire as before; first perform Dhara-homa, and then commence Vastu-homa.

Oblations should be offered to the Vastu-purusha and all his followers according to the best of one's ability. The sacrifice should be brought to a close by the gift of oblations to the Devas worshipped.

When Vastu-yajna is separately performed, this is the order which is prescribed, and in this order also the sacrifice to the planets should be performed.

Moreover, the Planets being the principal objects of worship, they should not be subordinately worshipped. The Vastu should be worshipped immediately after the sangkalpa.

Ganesha and the other Devas should be worshipped as in Vastu-yaga. I have already spoken to you of the Yantra and Mantra and Dhyana of the Planets.

I have, O Gentle One! during my discourse with thee spoken of the order to be observed in the yajnas of the planets and of Vastu. I shall now speak to thee of the various praiseworthy acts, beginning with the consecration of wells.

After making sangkalpa in the proper manner, Vastu should be worshipped either in a mandala, or a jar, or a Shilagrama, according to inclination.

Then Ganapati should be worshipped, as also Brahma and Vani, Hari, Rama, Shiva, Durga, the Planets, the Dikpatis.

Then the Matrikas and the eight Vasus having been worshipped, Pitrikriya should be performed. Since Varuna is principal Deva (for the purposes of this ceremony), he should then be worshipped with particular care.

Having worshipped Varuna with various presents to the best of his ability, Varuna Homa should then be performed in Fire duly consecrated. And after offering oblations to each of the Devas worshipped, he should bring the Homa rite to an end by giving the Purnahuti.

Then he should sprinkle the excellent well, decorated with flagstaffs and flags, garlands, scents, and vermilion, with the Prokshana Mantra, spoken of before.

Then he should, in the name of the Deva, or for the attainment of the object of his desire, give away the well or tank for the benefit of all beings.

Then the most excellent worshipper should make supplication with folded palms as follows:

"Be well pleased, all beings, whether living in the air or on earth or in water; I have given this excellent water to all beings; may all beings be satisfied by bathing in, drinking from, or plunging into this water; I have given this common water to all beings. Should anyone by his ownmisfortune be endangered in this, may I not be guilty of that sin, may my work (good work) bear fruit!".

Then presents should be made, and Shanti and other rites performed, and thereafter Brahmanas, Kaulas, and the hungry poor should be fed. Shive! this is the order to be observed in the consecration of all kinds of reservoirs of water.

In the consecration of a Tadaga and other kinds of reservoirs of water there should be a Nagastambha and some aquatic animals.

Aquatic animals, such as fish, frogs, alligators, and tortoises, should be made of metal, according to the means of the person consecrating. There should be made two fish and two frogs of gold, two alligators of silver, and two tortoises, one of copper and another of brass.

After giving away the Tadaga or Dirghika or Sagara with these aquatic animals, Naga should, after having been supplicated, be worshipped.

162

Ananta, Vasuki, Padma, Mahapadma, Takshaka, Kulira, Karkata, and Shankha – all these are the protectors of water.

These eight names of the Nagas should be written on Ashvattha leaves, and, after making japa of the Pranava and the Gayatri, the leaf should be thrown into a jar.

Calling upon Sun and Moon to witness, the leaves should be mixed up together, and one-half should be drawn therefrom, and the Naga whose name is drawn should be made the protector of water.

Then a wooden pillar, auspicious and straight, should be brought and smeared with oil and turmeric, and bathed in consecrated water, to the accompaniment of the Vyahriti and the Pranava, and then the Naga who has been made the protector of the water should be worshipped with the Shaktis Hri, Shri, Kshama, and Shanti.

Mantra

O Naga! Thou art the couch of Vishnu, Thou art the adornment of Shiva; do Thou inhabit this pillar and protect my water.

Having thus made supplication to Naga, the pillar should be set in the middle of the reservoir, and the dedicator should then go round the Tadaga, keeping it on his right.

If the pillar has been already fixed, then the Naga should be worshipped in a jar, and, throwing the water of the jar into the reservoir, the remainder of the rites should be performed.

Similarly, the wise man who has taken a vow to consecrate a house should perform the rites, beginning with the worship of Vastu, and ending with that of the Vasus, and perform the rites relating to the Pitris as prescribed for the consecration of a well, and the excellent devotee should worship Prajapati and do Prajapatya homa.

The house should be sprinkled with the Mantra already mentioned, and then worshipped with incense, etc.; after that, with his face to the Ishana corner, he should pray as follows:

Mantra

"O Room (or House)! Prajapati is thy Lord; decked with flowers and garlands and other decorations, be thou always pleasant for our happy residence.".

He should then offer presents, and, performing Shanti rites, accept blessings. Thereafter he should feed Vipras, Kulinas, and the poor to the best of his ability.

O Daughter of the Mountain! if the house is being consecrated for someone else, then in the place "our residence" should be said "their residence"; and now listen to the ordinances relating to the consecration of a house (or room) for a Deva.

After consecrating the house in the above manner, the Deva should be approached with the blowing of conch-shells and the sound of other musical instruments, and he should be supplicated thus:

Mantra

Rise, O Lord of the Deva among Devas! thou that grantest the desires of thy votaries! come and make my life blessed, O Ocean of Mercy!.

Having thus invited (the Deva) into the room, he should be placed at the door, and the Vahana should be placed in front of Him.

Then on the top of the house a trident or a discus should be placed, and in the Ishana corner a staff should be set with a flag flying from it.

Let the wise man then decorate the room with awnings, small bells, garlands of flowers, and mango-leaves, and then cover the house up with celestial cloth.

The Deva should be placed with his face to the North, and in the manner to be described he should be bathed with the things prescribed. I now am speaking of their order; do thou listen.

After saying Aing, Hring, Shring, the Mula Mantra should be repeated, and then let the worshipper say:

Mantra

I am bathing thee with milk; do thou cherish me like a mother.

Repeating the three Vijas and the Mula Mantra aforesaid, let him then say:

Mantra

I am bathing thee to-day with curds; do thou remove the heat of this mundane existence.

Repeating again the three Vijas and the Mula Mantra, let him say:

Mantra

O Giver of Joy to all! being bathed in honey, do Thou make me joyful.

Repeating the Mula Mantra as before, and inwardly reciting the Pranava and the Savitri, he should say:

Mantra

I am bathing Thee in ghee, which is dear to the Devas, which is longevity, seed, and courage; do Thou, O Lord! keep me free from disease.

Again repeating the Mula Mantra, as also the Vyahriti and the Gayatri, let him say:

Mantra

O Devesha ! bathed by me in sugar water, do Thou grant me (the object of) my desire.

Repeating the Mula Mantra, the Gayatri, and the Varuna Mantra, he should say:

Mantra

I am bathing thee with cocoanut-water, which is the creation of the Vidhi, which is divine, which is welcome to Devas, and is cooling, and which is not of the world; I bow to thee.

Then, with the Gayatri and the Mula Mantra, the Deva should be bathed with the juice of sugar-cane.

Repeating the Kama Vija and the Tara, the Savitri, and the Mula Mantra, he should, whilst bathing the Deva, say:

Mantra

Be thou well bathed in water scented with camphor, fragrant aloe, saffron, musk, and sandal; be thou pleased to grant me enjoyment and salvation.

After bathing the Lord of the World in this manner with eight jarfuls (of water, etc.), He should be brought inside the room and placed on His seat.

If the image be one which cannot be bathed, then the Yantra, or Mantra, or the Shalagrama-shila, should be bathed and worshipped.

If one be not able to bathe (the Deva) in manner above, then he should bathe (Him) with eight, seven, or five jars of pure water.

The size and proportions of the jar has been already given whilst speaking of Chakra worship. In all rites prescribed in the Agmas that is the jar which is appropriate.

Then the Great Deva should be worshipped according to the injunctions to be followed in His worship. I shall speak of the offerings. Do thou, O Supreme Devi! Listen.

A seat, welcome, water to wash the feet, offerings, water for rinsing the mouth, Madhuparka, water for sipping, bathing water, clothes and jewels, scents and flowers, lights and incense-sticks, edibles and words of praise, are the sixteen offerings requisite in the worship of the Devas.

Padya, Arghya, Achamana, Madhuparka, Achamya, Gandha, Pushpa, Dhupa, Dipa, Naivedya – these are known as Dashopachara (ten requisite offerings).

Gandha, Pushpa, Dhupa, Dipa, and Naivedya, are spoken of as the Panchopachara (five offerings) in the worship of a Deva.

The articles should be sprinkled with water taken from the offering with the Weapon Mantra, and be worshipped with scents and flowers, the names of separate articles being mentioned.

Mentally repeating the Mantra that is about to be said, as also the Mula Mantra, and the name of the Deva in the dative case, the words of gift should be repeated.

I have told you of the way in which the things to be given to the Devas should be dedicated. The learned man should in this manner give away an article to a Deva.

I have shown (whilst describing) the mode of worship of the Adya Devi how Padya, Arghya, etc., should be offered, and how Karana should be given.

To such of the Mantras as were not spoken then, do thou, O Beloved ! listen to them here; these should be said when Asana and other requisites are offered.

Mantra

(O Deva!) Thou who residest within all beings! who art the innermost of all beings! I am offering this seat for Thee to sit. I bow to Thee again and again.

O Deveshi! after giving the excellent asana in this way, the giver of the asana sbould with folded arms bid him welcome as follows:

Mantra

(O Deva!) Thou art He whom even the Devas seek for the accomplishment of their objects, yet for me Thy auspicious visit has easily been obtained. I bow to Thee, O Supreme Lord!.

My life's aim is accomplished to-day; all my efforts are crowned with success; I have obtained the fruits of my tapas – all this by Thy auspicious coming.

Ambika! the Deva should thus be invited, prayed to, and questioned as to His auspicious coming, and then, taking padya, the following Mantra should be repeated:

Mantra

By the mere touch of the washings of Thy feet the three worlds are purified; I am offering Thee padya for washing Thy lotus feet. He by whose grace is attained all manner of supreme bliss, to Him who is the Soul of all beings I offer this Anandarghya.

Then pure water which has been scented with nutmeg, cloves, and kakkola, should be poured out, and taken and offered with the following:

Mantra

(O Lord!) By the mere touch of that which Thou hast touched the whole of this impure world is purified; for washing that lotus mouth I offer thee this achamaniya.

Then, taking madhuparka, offer it with devotion and with the following:

Mantra

For the destruction of the three afflictions, for the attainment of uninterrupted bliss, I give Thee to-day, O Parameshvara! this madhuparka; be Thou propitious.

By the mere touch of anything which has touched Thy mouth things impure become pure: this punarachama-niyam is for the lotus mouth of Thine.

Taking water for the bath, and pouring it and consecrating it as before, it should be placed before the Deva, and the following Mantra should be repeated:

Mantra

To Thee whose splendour envelops the world, from whom the world was born, who is the support of the world, do I offer this water for Thy bath.

When offering bathing water, clothes, and edibles, achamaniya should be given as each is offered, and, after offering other articles, water should be given only once.

Bringing the cloth consecrated as aforementioned, holding it up with both hands, the wise man should repeat the following:

Mantra

Without any raiments as Thou art, Thou hast kept Thy splendour or glory concealed by Thy maya. To Thee I offer these two pieces of cloth. I bow to Thee.

Taking different kinds of ornaments made of gold and silver and other materials, and sprinkling and consecrating them, he should offer them to the Deva, uttering the following:

Mantra

To Thee who art the ornament of the Universe, who art the one cause of the beauty of the universe, I offer these jewels for the adornment of Thy illusion-image.

Mantra

To Thee who by the subtle element of smell hast created the earth which possesses all scents, to Thee, the Supreme Soul, I offer this excellent scent.

Mantra

By me have been dedicated with devotion beautiful flowers, and charming and sweet scents prepared by Devas: do Thou accept this fiower.

Mantra

This incense-stick is the sap of the trees; it is Divine, and possesses a delicious scent, and is charming, and is fit to be inhaled by all beings. I give it to Thee to smell.

Mantra

Do Thou accept this light which illumines and has a strong flame, which removes all darkness, and which is brightness itself, and makes bright that which is around it.

Mantra

This offering of food is of delicious taste, and consists of various kinds of edibles. I offer it to Thee in a devout spirit; do Thou partake of it.

Mantra

O Deva! this clear drinking-water, perfumed with camphor and other scents which satisfies all, I offer to Thee – Salutation to Thee.

The worshipper should then offer pan made with camphor, catechu, cloves, cardamums, and, after offering achamaniya, bow to Him.

If the offerings are presented along with the vessels in which they are contained, then the names and description of the offerings may jointly be repeated when making the present, or the names (or description) of the vessels may separately be said and the same given.

Having worshipped the Deva in this manner, three double handfuls of flowers should be given to the Deva. Then, sprinkling the temple and its awnings with water, the following Mantra should be said with folded palms:

Mantra

Temple! thou art adorable of all men; thou grantest virtue and fame. In affording a resting-place to this Deva, do thou be like unto Sumeru. Thou art Kailasa, thou art Vaikuntha, thou art the place of Brahma, since thou art holding the Deva, who is the adored of the Devas within thee.

Since thou holdest within thyself the image of Him whose body is produced by Maya, and within whose belly exists this universe, with all that is movable and immovable therein. Thou art the equal of the Mother of the Devas; all the holy places are in thee; do thou grant all my desires, and do thou bring me peace. I bow to thee.

Having thus praised the temple decorated with the discus, flag, etc., and worshipped it three times, the worshipper should give it to the Deva, mentioning the object of his desire.

Mantra

To Thee, whose abode is the universe for Thy residence, I dedicate this temple.O Maheshana! do Thou accept it and in Thy mercy abide here.

Having said this and having made presents, the Deva to whom the temple has been dedicated should be placed on the altar to the accompaniment of the music of conches, horns, and other instruments.

He should then touch the two feet of the Deva and utter the Mula Mantra, and say, Sthang! Sthing! be Thou steady; this temple is made by me for Thee, and, having fixed the Deva there, he should pray again to the temple thus:

Mantra

Temple! be thou always in every way pleasant for the residence of the Deva; thou hast been dedicated by me; may the Lokas be lasting and without danger for me.

Help my fourteen generations of ancestors, my fourteen generations of successors, and me and the rest of my family to find places to reside in the abode of the Devas.

May I, by thy grace, attain the fruits attainable by performing all forms of yajnas, by visiting all the places of pilgrimage.

May my line continue so long as this world, so long as these mountains, so long as the Sun and Moon endure.

The wise man, after having thus addressed the temple and worshipped the Deva, should dedicate mirrors and other articles and the flag to Him.

Then the Vahana appropriate to the Deity should be given. To Shiva should be given a bull. Then pray to Him thus:

Mantra

O Bull! thou art large of body, thy horns are sharp, thou killest all enemies, thou art worshipped even by the Tridashas, as thou carriest on thy back the Lord of the Devas.

In thy hoofs are all the holy shrines, in thy hair are all the Vedic Mantras, in the tip of thy teeth are all the Nigamas, Agamas, and Tantras.

May the husband of Parvati, pleased with this gift of thee, give me a place in Kailasa, and do thou protect me always.

O Maheshani! do Thou listen to the manner of prayer upon giving a lion to Mahadevi or a Garuda to Vishnu.

Mantra

Thou didst display thy great strength in the wars between the Suras and the Asuras; thou didst give victory to the Devas, and didst destroy the Demons. Thou formidable one, thou art the favourite of the Devi, thou the favourite of Brahma, Vishnu, and Shiva; with devotion I am dedicating thee to the Devi; do thou destroy my enemies. I bow to thee.

O Garuda! most excellent bird! Thou art the favoured one of the husband of Lakshmi; Thy beak is hard like adamant; Thy talons are sharp, and golder are Thy wings. I bow to Thee, O Indra among birds! I bow to Thee, O King of birds!.

As Thou abidest near Vishnu with folded palms, do Thou, O Destroyer of the pride of enemies! help me to be there as Thou art. When Thou art pleased, the Lord of the Universe is pleased, and grants success.

When a gift is made to any Deva, an additional present should be made to the Deva for His acceptance of such gifts, and the merit of such rites should also be given to Him in a spirit of devotion.

He should then, with dancing, singing, and music, go round the temple, accompanied by his friends and kinsmen, keeping the temple on his right, and, having bowed to the Deva, feed the twice-born!.

This is the way in which a temple to a Deva should be dedicated, and the same rule is to be observed in the dedication of a garden, a bridge, a causeway, or a tree.

With this difference only: that in these rites the ever-existing Vishnu should be worshipped; but Puja and Homa, etc., are the same as in the case of the dedication of a temple.

No temple or other thing should be dedicated to a Deva whose image has not been consecrated. The rules laid down above are for the worship of and dedication to a Deva who has been worshipped and consecrated.

I shall now speak of the manner in which the auspicious Adya should be installed, and by which the Devi grants quickly all desires.

On the morning of the day (of Pratishtha) the worshipper should, after bathing and purifying himself, sit facing the North, and, having taken Sangkalpa, worship the Vastu-devata.

After performing the worship of the planets, the Protectors of the Quarters, Ganesha and others, and having performed the Shraddha of his Pitris, he should approach the image with a number of devout Vipras.

The excellent worshipper should then bring the image to the temple which has been dedicated, or to some other place, and there duly bathe it.

It should first be bathed with water, then with sandy earth, then with mud thrown up by the tusk of the boar or elephant, then with mud taken from the door of a Veshya, and then with mud from the lake of Pradyumna.

The wise man should then bathe the image with Pancha-kashaya and Pancha-pushpa, and three leaves, and then with scented oil.

The decoctions of Vatyala, Vadari, Jambu, Vakula, and Shalmali, are called the five Kashayas for bathing the Devi.

Karavira, Jati, Champaka, Lotus, and Patali, are the five flowers.

By three leaves are meant the leaves of Varvvara, Tulasi, and Vilva.

With the above-mentioned articles water should be mixed, but no water should be put into scented oil and the five nectars.

He should, after repeating the Vyahriti, the Pranava, the Gayatri, and the Mula Mantra, say, "I bathe thee with the water of these articles".

The wise man should then bathe the image with the eight jars filled with milk and other ingredients in manners aforementioned.

The image should then be rubbed with powdered white wheat or sesamum cakes, or powdered shali rice, and thus cleansed.

After bathing the image with eight jars of holy water, and rubbing it with cloth of fine texture, it should bc brought to the place of worship.

Should one be unable to perform all these rites, then he should in a devout spirit bathe the image with twenty-five jars of pure water.

On each occasion that the Great Devi is bathed she should, to the best of one's ability, be worshipped.

Then, placing the image on a well-cleaned seat, She should be worshipped by offering padya, arghya, etc., and then prayed to (as follows):

Mantra

O Image! thou that art the handicraft of Vishvakarmma, I bow to thee; thou art the abode of the Devi, I bow to thee; thou fulfillest the desire of the votary, I bow to thee.

In thee I worship the most excellent primordial Supreme Devi; if there be any defect in thee by reason of the want of skill of him who has fashioned thee, do thou make it good; I bow to thee.

He should then restrain his speech, and, placing his hand over the head of the Image, inwardly do japa of the Mula Mantra one hundred and eight times, and thereafter do Anga-nyasa.

He should then perform Shadanga-nyasa and Matri-kanyasa on the body of the Image, and, when performing Shadanga-nyasa, add one after the other the six long vowels to the Vija.

The eight groups of the letters of the alphabet preceded by the Tara, Maya, and Rama, with the Vindu, added to them, and followed by Namah, should be placed in different parts of the body of the Deva.

The wise man should place the vowels in the mouth; kavarga in the throat; chavargaon the belly; tavarga on the right and tavarva on the left arm; pavarga on the right thigh, and yavarga on the left thigh, and shavarga on the head.

Having placed these groups of the letters of the alphabet on different parts of the image (the worshipper) should perform Tattva-nyasa (as follows):

Place on the two feet Prithivi-tattva; on the Linga Toya-tattva; on the region of the navel Tejas-tattva; on the lotus of the heart Vayu-tattva; on the mouth Gagana-tattva; on the two eyes Rupa-tattva; on the two nostrils Gandha-tattva; on the two ears Shabda-tattva; on the tongue Rasa-tattva; on the skin Sparsha-tattva. The foremost of worshippers should place Manas-tattva between the eyebrows, Shiva-tattva, Jnana-tattva, and Para-tattva on the lotus of a thousand petals; on the heart Jiva-tattva and Prakriti-tattva. Lastly, he should place Mahat-tattva and Ahangkara-tattva all over the body. The tattvas should, whilst being placed, be preceded by Tara, Maya, and Rama, and should be uttered in the dative singular, followed by namah.

Repeating the Mula Mantra, preceded and followed by each of the Matrika-varnas, with vindu added to them, and followed by the word namah, Matrika-nyasa should be performed at the Matrikasthanas. (The worshipper should then say):

Mantra

(Although) Thy radiance embraces all the sacrifices, and although Thy body embraces all being, this is the image that has been made of Thee. I place Thee here.

Thereafter the Devi should be meditated upon and invoked, according to the rules of worship, and after Prana-pratishtha the Supreme Devata should be worshipped.

The Mantras which are prescribed for the dedication of a temple to a Deva should be used in this ceremony, the necessary changes in gender being made.

The Devi should then be invoked into the fire, which has in due form been consecrated by the offer of oblations to the Devatas who are to be worshipped; and thereafter the Devi should be worshipped, and jata-karmma, etc., should be performed.

The Sangskaras are six in number – viz., Jatakarmma, Namakarana, Nishkramana, Annaprashana, Chudikarana, and Upanayana – this has been said by Shiva.

Repeating the Pranava, the Vyahritis, the Gayatri, the Mula Mantra, the worshipper used in the injunctions should say, "thine," and then the name of (the sangskara) jatakarmma, and others, and uttering, "I perform, Svaha," offer five oblations at the end of each sangskara.

Thereafter repeating the Mula Mantra and the name (given to the Devi), one hundred oblations should be offered, and the remnants of each oblation should be thrown over the head of the Devi.

The wise man, after having brought the ceremony to a close by Prayashchitta and other rites, should feed and thus please Sadhakas and Vipras and the poor and the helpless.

Should anyone be unable to perform all these rites, he should bathe (the Deva) with seven jars of water, and, having worshipped to the best of his ability, repeat the name of the Devi.

Beloved! I have now spoken to Thee of the Pratishtha of the illustrious Adya. In a similar way should men versed in the regulations carefully perform the Pratishtha of Durga and other Vidyas, Mahesha, and other Devatas, and of the Shiva-lingas that may be moved.

End of the Thirteenth Joyful Message, entitled "Installation of the Devata."

Chapter 14

The Consecration of Shiva-linga and Description of the Four Classes of Avadhutas

SHRI DEVI said:

I am grateful to Thee, O Lord of Mercy! in that Thou hast in Thy discourse upon the Worship of the Adya Shakti, spoken, in Thy mercy, of the mode of Worship of various other Devas.

Thou hast spoken of the Installation of a Movable Shiva-linga, but what is the object of installing an immovable Shiva-linga, and what are the rites relating to the installation of such a Linga?.

Do Thou, O Lord of the Worlds! now tell Me all the particulars thereof; for say, who is there but Thee that I can honour by My questions anent this excellent subject?.

Who is there that is Omniscient, Merciful, All-knowing, Omnipresent, easily satisfied, Protector of the humble, like Thee? Who makes My joys increase like Thee?.

Shri Sadashiva said:

What shall I tell Thee of the merit acquired by the installation of a Shiva-linga? By it a man is purified of all great sins, and goes to the Supreme Abode.

There is no doubt that by the installation of a Shiva-linga a man acquires ten million times the merit which is acquired by giving the world and all its gold, by the performance of ten thousand horse-sacrifices, by the digging of a tank in a waterless country, or by making happy the poor and such as are enfeebled by disease.

Kalika! Brahma, Vishnu, Indra, and the other Devas reside where Mahadeva is in His linga form.

Thirty-five million known and unknown places of pilgrimage and all the holy places abide near Shiva. The land within a radius of a hundred cubits of the linga is declared to be Shiva-kshetra.

This land of Isha is very sacred. It is more excellent than the most excellent of holy places, because there abide all the Immortals and there are all the holy places.

He who in a devout spirit lives there, be it even for but a little while, becomes purged of all sins, and goes to the heaven of Shangkara after death.

Anything great or small (meritorious or otherwise) which is done in this land of Shiva becomes multiplied (in its effect) by the majesty of Shiva.

All sins committed elsewhere are removed (by going) near Shiva, but sins committed in Shiva-kshetra adhere to a man with the strength of a thunderbolt.

The merit acquired by the performance there of Purashcharana, japa, acts of charity, Shraddha, tarpana, or any other pious acts is eternal.

The merit acquired by the performance of a hundred Purashcharana at times of lunar or solar eclipse is acquired by merely performing one japa near Shiva.

By the offering of Pinda once only in the land of Shiva, a man obtains the same fruit as he who offers ten million pindas at Gaya, the Ganges, and Prayaga.

Even in the case of those who are guilty of many sins or of great sins attain the supreme abode if Shraddha be performed in their names in the land of Shiva.

The fourteen worlds abide there where abides the Lord of the Universe in His Linga form with the auspicious Devi Durga.

I have spoken a little about the majesty of the immovable Mahadeva in His linga form. The mahima of the Anadi-linga is beyond the power of words to express.

O Suvrat! even in Thy worship at the Mahapithas the touch of an untouchable is unclean, but this is not so in the worship of Hara in His linga image.

O Devi! as there are no prohibitions at the time of Chakra worship, so know this, O Kalika! that there are none in the holy shrine in Shiva's land.

What is the use of saying more? I am but telling Thee the very truth when I say that I am unable to describe the glory, majesty, and sanctity of the linga image of Shiva.

Whether the Linga is placed on a Gauri-patta or not, the worshipper should, for the successful attainment of his desires, worship it devoutly.

The excellent worshipper earns the merit of (performing) ten thousand horse-sacrifices if he performs the Adhivasa of the Deva in the evening previous to the day of installation.

The twenty articles to be used in the rite of Adhivasa are: Earth, Scent, a Pebble, Paddy, Durvva grass, Flower, Fruit, Curds, Ghee, Svastika, Vermillion, Conch-shell, Kajjala, Rochana, White Mustard Seed, Silver, Gold, Copper, Lights, and a Mirror.

Taking each of these articles, the Maya Vija and the Brahma-Gayatri should be repeated, and then should be said "Anena" (with this) and "Amushya" (of this one's or his or hers) – "may the auspicious Adhivasa be".

And then the forehead of the worshipped divinity should be touched with the earth and all other articles aforesaid. Then Adhivasa should be performed with the Prashasti-patra – that is, the receptacle should be lifted up, and with it the forehead of the image should be touched three times.

The worshipper conversant with the ordinances, having thus performed the Adhivasa of the Deva, should bathe the deity with milk and other liquids, as directed in the ceremony relating to the dedication of a temple.

Rubbing the linga with a piece of cloth and placing it on its seat, Ganesha and other Deities should be worshipped according to the rules prescribed for their worship.

Having performed Kara-nyasa and Anga-nyasa and Pranayama with the Pranava, the ever-existent Shiva should be meditated upon.

Dhyana

As tranquil, possessed of the effulgence of ten million Moons; clothed in garments of tiger-skins; wearing a sacred thread made of a serpent; His whole body covered with ashes; wearing ornaments of serpents; His five faces are of reddish-black, yellow, rose, white, and red colours, with three eyes each; His head is covered with matted hair; He is Omnipresent; He holds Ganga on His head, and has ten arms, and in His forehead shines the (crescent) Moon; He holds in His left hand the skull, fire, the noose, the Pinaka, and the axe, and in His right the trident, the thunderbolt, the arrow, and blessings; He is being praised by all the

Devas and great Sages; His eyes half-closed in the excess of bliss; His body is white as the snow and the Kunda flower and the Moon; He is seated on the Bull; He is by day and night surrounded on every side by Siddhas, Gandharvas, and Apsaras, who are chanting hymns in His praise; He is the husband of Uma; the devoted Protector of His worshippers.

Having thus meditated upon Mahadeva and worshipped Him with articles of mental worship, He should be invoked into the Linga, and worshipped to the best of one's powers, and as laid down in the ordinances relating to such worship.

I have already spoken of the Mantras for the giving of Asana and other articles of worship. I shall now speak of the Mula Mantra of the Great Mahesha.

Maya, Tara, and the Shabda Vija, with Au and Ardhendu-Vindu added to it, is the Shiva Vija – that is, "Hring Ong Haung.".

Covering Shangkara with clothes and garland of sweet-smelling flowers, and placing Him on a beautiful couch, the Gauri-patta should be consecrated in manner above-mentioned.

The Devi should be worshipped in the Gauri-patta according to the following rites: with the Maya Vija, Anga-nyasa, Kara-nyasa, and Pranayama should be performed.

The Great Devi should, to the best of the worshipper's ability, be worshipped after meditation upon Her as follows:

Dhyana

I meditate upon the stainless One, Whose splendour isthat of a thousand rising Suns, Whose eyes are like Fire, Sun and Moon, and Whose lotus face in smiles is adorned with golden earrings set with lines of pearls. With her lotus hands She makes the gestures which grant blessings and dispel fear, and holds the discus and lotus; Her breasts are large and rounded; She is the Dispeller of all fear, and She is clothed in saffron-coloured raiments.

Having thus meditated upon Her, the ten Dikpalas and the Bull should be worshipped to the best of one's powers.

I will now speak of the Mantra of the Bhagavati, by which the World-pervading One should be worshipped.

Repeating the Maya, Lakshmi Vijas, and the letter which follows Sa with the sixth vowel, with the Vindu added to it, and thereafter uttering the name of the Wife of Fire, the Mantra is formed (which is as follows):

Mantra

Hring Shring Hung Svaha.

Placing the Devi as aforementioned, offerings should be made to all the Devas with a mixture of Masha beans, rice, and curds, with sugar, etc., added to it.

These articles of worship should be placed in the Ishana corner, and purified with the Varuna Vija, and should be offered after purification with scents and flowers and the following

Mantra

O Devas, Siddhas, Gandharvas, Uragas, Rakshasas, Pishachas,' Mothers, Yakshas, Bhutas, Pitris, Rishis, and other Devas! do you quietly take this offering, and do you stay surrounding Mahadeva and Girija.

Then japa should be made of the Mantra of the Great Devi as often as one may, and then with excellent songs and instrumental music let the festival be celebrated.

Having completed the Adhivasa in manner above, the following day after performance of the compulsory daily duties, and having taken the vow, the Five Devas should be worshipped.

After worshipping the Matris and making the Vasudhara, and performing Vriddhi-Shraddha, the Door-keepers of Mahesha should, in a calm and devout frame of mind, be worshipped.

The Door-keepers of Shiva are – Nandi, Maha-bala, Kishavadana, and Gana-nayaka; they are all armed with missiles and other weapons.

Bringing the Linga and Tarini, as represented by the Gauri-patta, they should be placed on a Sarvato-bhadra Mandala, or on an auspicious seat.

Shambhu should then be bathed with eight jars of water with the Mantra "Tryambaka," etc., and worshipped with the sixteen articles of worship.

After bathing the Devi in a similar way with the Mula Mantra, and worshipping Her, the good worshipper should pray to Shangkara with joined palms.

Mantra

Come, O Bhagavan! O Shambhu! O Thou before Whom all Devas bow! I bow to Thee, Who art armed with the Pinaka, Thee the Lord of all, O Great Deva.

O Deva! Thou Who conferrest benefits on Thy votaries! do Thou in Thy mercy come to this temple with Bhagavati: I bow to Thee again and again.

O Mother! O Devi! O Mahamaya! O All-beneficent One! be Thou along with Shambhu pleased: I bow to Thee, O Beloved of Hara.

Come to this house, O Devi! Thou Who grantest all boons, be Thou pleased, and do Thou grant me all prosperity.

Rise, O Queen of Devas! and Each with Thy followers abide happy in this place; may Both of You be pleased, You Who are kind to your devotees.

Having thus prayed to Shiva and the Devi, They should first be carried three times round the Temple, keeping the latter on the right to the accompaniment of joyful sounds, and then taken inside.

Repeating the Mula Mantra, one-third of the Linga should be set in a hollow made in a piece of stone or in a masonry hole. (With the following Mantra):

Mantra

O Mahadeva! do Thou remain here so long as the Moon and the Sun endure, so long as the Earth and the Oceans endure: I bow to Thee.

Having firmly fixed Sadashiva with this Mantra, the Gauri-patta, with its tapering end to the North, should be placed on the Linga, that it may be entered by the latter.

Mantra

Be still, O Jagad-dhatri! Thou That art the Cause of creation, existence, and destruction of things; abide Thou here so long as the Sun and the Moon endure.

Having firmly fixed it, the Linga should be touched and the following (Mantra) should be repeated:

Mantra

I invoke that Deva Who has three eyes, the Decayless, Ishana, around whose lion-seat are tigers, Bhutas, Pishachas, Gandharvas, Siddhas, Charanas, Yakshas, Nagas, Vetalas, Loka-palas, Maharshis, Matris, Gana-nathas, Vishnu Brahma, and Vrihaspati, and all beings which live on earth or in the air; come, O Bhagavan! to this Yantra, which is the handiwork of Brahma, for the prosperity, happiness, and Heaven of all.

Beloved! Shiva should then be bathed according to the injunctions relating to the consecration of a Deva, and, having been meditated upon as before-mentioned, should be worshipped with mental offerings.

After placing a special arghya,' and having worshipped the Gana-devatas, and meditated upon Mabesha again, flowers should be placed on the Linga.

Repeating the Shakti Vija between Pasha and Angkusha, and the letters from Ya to Sa with the nasal point, and then " Haung Hangsa," the life of Sadashiva should be infused into the Linga.

Then, smearing the Husband of the Daughter of the Mountain with sandal, aguru, and saffron, He should be worshipped with the sixteen articles of worship according to the injunctions laid down after performing the jata, the nama, and other rites.

After concluding everything according to the injunctions, and after worshipping the Devi in the Gauri-patta, the eight images of the Deva should be carefully worshipped.

By the name Sharva the Earth is meant; by Bhava is meant Water; by Rudra, Fire; by Ugra, Wind; by Bhuna, Ether; by Pashu-pati is meant the Employer of a priest for sacrifice; by Mahadeva, the Source of Nectar, and by Ishana, the Sun: these are declared to be the Eight Images.

Each of these should be invoked and worshipped in their order (in the corners), beginning with the East and ending with the North-East, uttering the Pranava first and Namah last.

After having worshipped Indra and the other Dikpalas, the eight Matris, Brahmi, and others, the worshipper should give to Isha the Bull, awning, houses, and the like.

Then, with joined palms, he should with fervour pray to the Husband of Parvati (as follows):

Mantra

O Ocean of Mercy! O Lord! Thou hast been placed in this place by me; be Thou pleased (with me). O Shambhu! Thou Who art the Cause of all causes, do Thou abide in this room, O Supreme Deva! so long as the Earth with all its Oceans exist, so long as the Moon and the Sun endure. I bow to Thee. Should there occur the death of any living being, may I, O Dhurjjati! by Thy grace, be kept from that sin.

The dedicator should go round the image, keeping it on his right, and, having bowed before the Deva, go home. Returning again in the morning, he should bathe Chandra-Shekhara.

181

He should first be bathed with consecrated Panchamrita with a hundred jars of scented water, and the worshipper, having worshipped Him to the best of his powers, should pray to Him (as follows):

Mantra

O Husband of Uma,! if there has been any irregularity, omission, want of devotion in this worship, may they all, by Thy grace, be rectified, and may my fame remain incomparable in this world so long as Moon, the Sun, the Earth, and its Oceans endure.

I bow to the three-eyed Rudra, Who wields the excellent Pinaka, to Him Who is worshipped by Vishnu, Brahma, Indra, Suryya, and other Devas, I bow again and again.

The worshipper should then make presents, and feast the Kaulika-dvijas, and give pleasure to the poor by gifts of food, drink, and clothes.

The Deva should be worshipped every day according to one's means. The fixed Shiva-linga should on no account be removed.

Parameshvari! I have in brief spoken to you of the rites relating to the consecration of the immovable Shiva-linga, gathering same from all the Agamas.

Shri Devi said:

If, O Lord! there be an accidental omission in the worship of the Devas, then what should be done by their votaries – do Thou speak in detail about this.

Say, on account of what faults are images of Devas unfit for worship, and should thus be rejected, and what should be done?.

Shri Sadashiva said:

If there be an omission to worship an image for a day, then (the next day) the worship should be twice performed; if for two days, then the worship should be four times performed; if for three days, then it should be celebrated eight times.

If the omission extends three days, but does not exceed six months, then the wise man should worship after bathing the Deva with eight jars of water.

If the period of omission exceeds six months, then the excellent worshipper should carefully consecrate the Deva according to the rules already laid down, and then worship Him

The wise man should not worship the image of a Deva which is broken or is holed, or which has lost a limb, or has been touched by a leper, or has fallen on unholy ground.

The image of a Deva with missing limbs, or which is broken or has holes in it, should be consigned to water. If the image has been made impure by touch, it should be consecrated, and then worshipped.

The Mahapithas and Anadi-lingas are free from all deficiencies, and these should always be worshipped for the attainment of happiness by each worshipper as he pleases.

Mahamaya! whatever Thou hast asked for the good of men who act with a view to the fruits of action, I have answered all this in detail.

Men cannot live without such actions even for half amoment. Even when men are unwilling, they are, in spite of themselves, drawn by the whirlwind of action.

By action men enjoy happiness, and by action again they suffer pain. They are born, they live, and they die the slaves of action.

It is for this that I have spoken of various kinds of action, such as S,dhana and the like, for the guidance of the intellectually weak in the paths of righteousness, and that they may be restrained from wicked acts.

There are two kands of action – good and evil; the effect of evil action is that men suffer acute pain.

And, O Devi! those who do good acts with minds intent on the fruits thereof go to the next world, and come back again to this, chained by their action.

Therefore men will not attain final liberation even at the end of a hundred kalpas so long as action, whether good or evil, is not destroyed.

As a man is bound, be it by a gold or iron chain, so he is bound by his action, be it good or evil.

So long as a man has not real knowledge, he does not attain final liberation, even though he be in the constant practice of religious acts and a hundred austerities.

The knowledge of the wise from whom the darkness of ignorance is removed, and whose souls are pure, arises from the performance of duty without expectation of fruit or reward, and by constant meditation on the Brahman.

He who knows that all which is in this universe from Brahma to a blade of grass is but the result of Maya, and that the Brahman is the one and supreme Truth, has this.

That man is released from the bonds of action who, renouncing name and form, has attained to complete knowledge of the essence of the eternal and immutable Brahman.

Liberation does not come fram japa, homa, or a hundred fasts; man becomes liberated by the knowledge that he himself is Brahman.

Final liberation is attained by the knowledge that the Atma (Soul) is the witness, is the Truth, is omnipresent, is one, free from all illuding distractions of self and not-self, the supreme, and, though abiding in the body, is not in the body.

All imagination of name-form and the like are but the play of a child. He who put away all this sets himself in firm attachment to the Brahman, is, without doubt, liberated.

If the image imagined by the (human) mind were to lead to liberation, then undoubtedly men would be Kings by virtue of such kingdoms as they gain in their dreams.

Those who (in their ignorance) believe that Ishvara is (only) in images made of clay, or stone, or metal, or wood, merely trouble themselves by their tapas. They can never attain liberation without knowledge.

Can men attain final liberation by restriction in food, be they ever so thin thereby, or by uncontrolled indulgence, be they ever so gross therefrom, unless they possess the knowledge of Brahman?.

If by observance of Vrata to live on air, leaves of trees, bits of grain, or water, final liberation may be attained, then snakes, cattle, birds, and aquatic animals should all be able to attain final liberation.

Brahma-sad-bhava is the highest state of mind; dhyana-bhava is middling; stuti and japa is the last; and external worship is the lowest of all.

Yoga is the union of the embodied soul and the Supreme Soul," Puja is the union of the worshipper and the worshipped; but he who realizes that all things are Brahman for him there is neither Yoga nor Puja.

For him who possesses the knowledge of Brahman, the supreme knowledge, of what use are japa, yajna," tapas, niyama, and vrata?.

He who sees the Brahman, Who is Truth, Knowledge, Bliss, and the One, is by his very nature one with the Brahman. Of what use to him are puja, dhyana, and dharana?.

For him who knows that all is Brahman there is neither sin nor virtue, neither heaven nor future birth. There is none to meditate upon, nor one who meditates.

The soul which is detached from all things is ever liberated; what can bind it? From what do fools desire to be liberated?.

He abides in this Universe, the creation of His powers of illusion, which even the Devas cannot pierce. He is seemingly in the Universe, but not in it.

The Spirit, the eternal witness, is in its own nature like the void which exists both outside and inside all things, and which has neither birth nor childhood, nor youth nor old age, but is the eternal intelligence which is ever the same, knowing no change or decay.

It is the body which is born, matures, and decays. Men enthralled by illusion, seeing this, understand it not.

As the Sun (though one and the same) when reflected in different platters of water appears to be many, so by illusion the one soul appears to be many in the different bodies in which it abides.

As when water is disturbed the Moon which is reflected in it appears to be disturbed, so when the intelligence is disturbed ignorant men think that it is the soul which is disturbed.

As the void inside a jar remains the same ever after the jar is broken, so the Soul remains the same after the body is destroyed.

The knowledge of the Spirit, O Devi! is the one means of attaining final liberation; and he who possesses it is verily – yea, verily – liberated in this world, even yet whilst living, there is no doubt of that.

Neither by acts, nor by begetting offspring, nor by wealth is man liberated; it is by the knowledge of the Spirit, by the Spirit that man is liberated.

It is the Spirit that is dear to all; there is nothing dearer than the Spirit;O Shive! it is by the unity of Spirits that men become dear to one another.

Knowledge, Object of knowledge, the knower appear by illusion to be three different things; but if careful discrimination is made, Spirit is found to be the sole residuum.

Knowledge is Spirit in the form of intelligence, the object of knowledge is Spirit whose substance is intelligence, the Knower is the Spirit Itself. He who knows this knows the Spirit.

I have now spoken of knowledge which is the true cause of final liberation. This is the most precious possession of the four classes of Avadhutas.

Shri Devi said:

Thou hast spoken of the two stages in the life of man – namely, that of householder and mendicant; what is this wonderful distinction of four classes of Avadhutas which I now hear?.

I wish to hear and clearly understand the distinctive features of the four classes of Avadhutas: do Thou, O Lord! speak (about them) truly.

Shri Sadashiva said:

Those Brahmanas, Kshatriyas, and other castes who are worshippers of the Brahma-mantra should be known to be Yatis, even though they be living the life of a householder.

O Worshipped of the Kulas! those men who are sanctified by the rites of Purnabhisheka should be known and honoured as Shaivavadhutas.

Both the Brahma and Shaiva Avadhutas shall do all acts in their respective states of life according to the way directed by me.

They should not partake of forbidden food or drink unless the same has been offered to the Brahman or offered in the Chakra.

O Beauteous One! I have already spoken of the customs and Dharmma of the Kaulas, who are Brahma Avadhutas, and of the Kaulas who have been initiated. For Brahma and Shaiva Avadhutas, bathing, eating evening meals, drinking, the giving of charities, and marital intercourse should be done according to the way prescribed by the Agamas.

The above Avadhutas are of two classes, according as they are perfect or imperfect. Beloved! the perfect one is called Parama-hangsa, and the other or imperfect one is called Parivrat.

The man who has gone through the Sangskara of an Avadhuta, but whose knowledge is yet imperfect, should, by living the life of a householder, purify his spirit.

Preserving his caste-mark and practising the rites of a Kaula, he should, remaining constantly devoted to the Brahman, cultivate the excellent knowledge.

With his mind ever free from attachment, yet discharging all his duty, he should constantly repeat "Ong Tat Sat," and constantly think upon and realize the saying, "Sah aham".

Doing his duties, his mind as completely detached as the water on the lotus leaf, he should constantly strive to free his soul by the knowledge of Divine truth and discrimination.

The man, be he a householder or an ascetic, who commences any undertaking with the Mantra "Ong Tat Sat," is ever successful therein.

Japa, homa, pratishtha, and all sacramental rites, if performed with the Mantra "Ong Tat Sat," are faultess beyond all doubt.

What use is there of the various other Mantras? What use of the other multitudinous practices? With this Brahma Mantra alone may all rites be concluded.

Ambika! this Mantra is easily practised, is not prolix, and gives complete success, and there is no other way besides this great Mantra.

If it be kept written in any part of the house or on the body, then such house becomes a holy place and the body becomes sanctified.

O Deveshi! I am telling Thee the very truth when I say that the Mantra "Ong Tat Sat" is superior to the essence of essences of the Nigamas, the Agamas, and the Tantras.

This most excellent of Mantras, "Ong Tat Sat," has pierced through the palate, the skull, and crownlock of Brahma, Vishnu, and Shiva, and has thus manifested itself.

If the four kinds of food and other articles are sanctified by this Mantra, then it becomes useless to sanctify them by any other Mantras.

He is a King among Kaulas, who sees the Great Being everywhere, and constantly makes japa of the great Mantra "Tat Sat" (i.e., Ong Tat Sat), acts as he so inclines, and is pure of heart withal.

By japa of this Mantra a man becomes a Siddha; by thinking of its meaning he is liberated, and he who, when making japa, thinks of its meaning, becomes like unto the Brahman in visible form.

This Great, Three-footed Mantra is the cause of all causes; by its sadhana one becomes the Conqueror of Death himself.

O Maheshani! the worshipper attains siddhi in whatsoever way he makes japa of it.

He who, renouncing all acts (rites), has been cleansed by the Sangskara of a Shaiva Avadhuta, ceases to have any right to worship Devas, to perform the Shraddha of the Pitris, or to honour the Rishis.

Of the four classes of Avadhutas, the fourth is called the Hangsa (Parama-hangsa). The other three both practise yoga and have enjoyment. They are all liberated and are like unto Shiva.

The Hangsa should not have intercourse with women, and should not touch metals. Unfettered by restrictions, he moves about enjoying the fruits of his meritorious acts done in previous lives.

The fourth class, removing his caste-marks and relinquishing his household duties, should move about in this world without aim or striving.

Always pleased in his own mind, he is free from sorrow and illusion, homeless and forgiving, fearless, and doing harm to none.

For him there is no offering of food and drink (to any Deva); for him there is no necessity for dhyana or dharana, the Yati is liberated, is free from attachment, unaffected by all opposites, and follows the ways of a Hangsa.

O Devi! I have now spoken to Thee in detail of the distinctive marks of the four classes of Kula-Yogis, who are but images of Myself.

By seeing them, by touching them, conversing with them, or pleasing them, men earn the fruit of pilgrimage to all the holy places.

All the shrines and holy places which there are in this world, they all, O my Beloved! abide in the body of the Kula-Sannyasi.

Those men who have worshipped Kula Sadhus with

Kula-dravya are indeed blessed and holy, have attained their desired aim, and have earned the fruit of all sacrifices.

By mere touch of these Sadhus the impure becomes pure, the untouchable becomes touchable, and food unfit to be eaten becomes fit to be eaten. By their touch even the Kiratas, the sinful, the wicked, the Pulindas, the Yavanas, and the wicked and ferocious, are made pure; who else but they should be honoured?.

Even those who but once worship the Kaulika Yogi with Kula-tattva and Kula-dravya become worthy of honour in this world.

O Thou with the lotus face! there is no Dharmma superior to Kaula-Dharmma, by seeking refuge in which even a man of inferior caste becomes purified and attains the state of a Kaula.

As the footmarks of all animals disappear in the footmark of the elephant, so do all other Dharmmas disappear in the Kula-Dharmma.

My Beloved! how holy are the Kaulas! They are like the images of the holy places. They purify by their merepresence even the Chandalas and the vilest of the vile.

As other waters falling into Ganga become the water of Ganga, so all men following Kulachara reach the stage of a Kaula.

As water gone into the sea does not retain its separateness, so men sunk in the ocean of Kula lose theirs.

All beings in this world which have two feet, from the Vipra to the inferior castes, are competent for Kulachara.

Those that are averse to the acceptance of Kula-Dharmma, even when invited, are divorced from all Dharmma and go the downward path.

The Kulina who deceived those men who seek for Kulachara shall go to the hell named Raurava.

That low Kaula who refuses to initiate a Chandala or a Yavana into the Kula-Dharmma, considering them to be inferior, or a woman out of disrespect for her, goes the downward way.

The merit acquired by a hundred Abhisheka, by the performance of a hundred Purashcharana, ten million times that merit is acquired by the initiation of one man into the Kula-Dharmma.

All the different castes, all the followers of the different Dharmmas in this world, are, by becoming Kaulas, freed from their bonds, and go to the Supreme Abode.

The Kaulas who follow that Shaiva-Dharmma are like places of pilgrimage, and possess the soul of Shiva. They worship and honour one another with affection, respect, and love.

What is the use of saying more? I am speaking the very truth before Thee when I say that the only bridge for the crossing of this ocean of existence is the Kula- Dharmma and none other.

By the following of Kula-Dharmma all doubts are cut through, all the accumulation of sins is destroyed, and the multitude of acts is destroyed.

Those Kaulikas are excellent who, truthful and faithful to the Brahman, in their mercy invite men to purify them by Kulachara.

Devi! I have spoken to Thee the first portion of the Maha-nirvana Tantra for the purification of men. It contains the conclusions of all Dharmmas.

He who hears it daily or enables other men to hear it becomes freed from all sins, and attains Nirvana at the end.

By knowing this King among Tantras, which contains the essence of essence of all the Tantras, and is the most excellent among the Tantras, a man becomes versed in all the Shastras.

The man who knows this Maha-Tantra is freed fromthe bonds of actions. Of what use is it to him to go on pilgrimage, or to do japa, yajna, and sadhana?.

Kalika! he who knows this Tantra, is conversant with all the Shastras, he is pre-eminent among the virtuous, is wise, knows the Brahman, and is a Sage.

There is no use of the Vedas, the Puranas, the Smritis,. the Sanghitas, and the various other Tantras, as by knowing this Tantra one knows all.

All the most secret rites and practices and the most excellent knowledge have been revealed by me in reply to Thy questions.

Suvrata! as Thou art my most excellent Brahmi Shakti, and art to me dearer than life itself, know Thou that the Mahanirvana Tantra is likewise.

As the Himalaya is among the Mountains, as the Moon is among the Stars, as the Sun is among all lustrous bodies, so this Tantra is the King among Tantras.

All the Dharmmas pervade this Tantra. It is the only means for the acquirement of the knowledge of Brahman. The man who repeats himself or causes others to repeat it will surely acquire such knowledge.

In the family of the man in whose house there is this most excellent of all Tantras there will never be a Pashu.

The man blinded by the darkness of ignorance, the fool caught in the meshes of his actions, and the illiterate man, by listening to this Great Tantra, are released fromthe bonds of karmma.

Parameshani! reading, listening to, and worshipping this Tantra, and singing its praise, gives liberation to men.

Of the other various Tantras each deals with one subject only. There is no other Tantra which contains all the Dharmmas.

The last part contains an account of the nether, earthly, and heavenly worlds. He who knows it (along with the first) undoubtedly knows all.

The man who knows the second part with this book is able to speak of the past, present, and future, and knows the three worlds.

There are all manner of Tantras and various Shastras, but they are not equal to a sixteenth part (in value) of this Mahanirvana Tantra.

What further shall I tell Thee of the greatness of the Mahanirvana Tantra? Through the knowledge of it one shall attain to Brahma-nirvana.

Other books from

Freemasonry

Look to the East
- Ralph P. Lester
Morals and Dogma
- Albert Pike
Duncan's Ritual and Monitor of Freemasonry
- Malcolm C. Duncan
Ritual of the Order of the Eastern Star
- F. A. Bell
Meaning of Masonry
- W.L Wilmshurst
Exposition of Freemasonry – Illustrated
- WM. Morgan

Philosophy

Politics
- Aristotle
Republic
- Plato
The Advancement of Learning
- Francis Bacon
The Interpretation of Dreams
- Sigmund Freud
HAGAKURE - Selections (The Way of the Samurai)
- Yamamoto Tsunetomo

Autobiographys

Autobiography of Ben Franklin
Autobiography of Charles Darwin
Autobiography of John Stuart Mill

Religious

Book of Jasher
- J.H. Parry
The Way to Christ
- Jacob Boehme
Imitation of Christ
- Thomas A Kempis
The First Book of Adam and Eve
- Rutherford H. Platt

Miscellaneous

The Devil's Dictionary
- Ambrose Bierce
Ancient Egypt - The Light of the World
- Gerald Massey
Natural Magick
- John Baptista Porta
The Two Babylons
- Alexander Hislop

And many, many more titles available at

www.nuvisionpublications.com

Lightning Source UK Ltd.
Milton Keynes UK
UKOW040639280213

206953UK00001B/65/A